How to Open & Operate a Financially Successful

Pet Sitting Business

With Companion CD-ROM

By Angela Williams Duea

How to Open & Operate a Financially Successful Pet Sitting Business — With Companion CD-ROM

1405 SW 6th Ave. • Ocala, Florida 34471 • 800-814-1132 • 352-622-1875–Fax
Web site: www.atlantic-pub.com • E-mail: sales@atlantic-pub.com
SAN Number: 268-1250

ISBN-13: 978-1-60138-229-0 ISBN-10: 1-60138-229-4

Library of Congress Cataloging-in-Publication Data

Williams Duea, Angela, 1966-
How to open & operate a financially successful pet sitting business : with companion CD-ROM / by Angela Williams Duea.
p. cm.
Includes bibliographical references and index.
ISBN-13: 978-1-60138-229-0 (alk. paper)
ISBN-10: 1-60138-229-4 (alk. paper)
1. Pet sitting. 2. New business enterprises. I. Title. II. Title: How to open and operate a financially successful pet sitting business.

SF414.34.W55 2008
636.088'7--dc22

2008014105

INTERIOR LAYOUT DESIGN: Vickie Taylor • vtaylor@atlantic-pub.com

Printed in the United States

Printed on Recycled Paper

We recently lost our beloved pet "Bear," who was not only our best and dearest friend but also the "Vice President of Sunshine" here at Atlantic Publishing. He did not receive a salary but worked tirelessly 24 hours a day to please his parents. Bear was a rescue dog that turned around and showered myself, my wife Sherri, his grandparents Jean, Bob and Nancy and every person and animal he met (maybe not rabbits) with friendship and love. He made a lot of people smile every day.

We wanted you to know that a portion of the profits of this book will be donated to The Humane Society of the United States.

–Douglas & Sherri Brown

THE HUMANE SOCIETY OF THE UNITED STATES©

The human-animal bond is as old as human history. We cherish our animal companions for their unconditional affection and acceptance. We feel a thrill when we glimpse wild creatures in their natural habitat or in our own backyard.

Unfortunately, the human-animal bond has at times been weakened. Humans have exploited some animal species to the point of extinction.

The Humane Society of the United States makes a difference in the lives of animals here at home and worldwide. The HSUS is dedicated to creating a world where our relationship with animals is guided by compassion. We seek a truly humane society in which animals are respected for their intrinsic value, and where the human-animal bond is strong.

Want to help animals? We have plenty of suggestions. Adopt a pet from a local shelter, join The Humane Society and be a part of our work to help companion animals and wildlife. You will be funding our educational, legislative, investigative and outreach projects in the U.S. and across the globe.

Or perhaps you'd like to make a memorial donation in honor of a pet, friend or relative? You can through our Kindred Spirits program. And if you'd like to contribute in a more structured way, our Planned Giving Office has suggestions about estate planning, annuities, and even gifts of stock that avoid capital gains taxes.

Maybe you have land that you would like to preserve as a lasting habitat for wildlife. Our Wildlife Land Trust can help you. Perhaps the land you want to share is a backyard—that's enough. Our Urban Wildlife Sanctuary Program will show you how to create a habitat for your wild neighbors.

So you see, it's easy to help animals. And The HSUS is here to help.

The Humane Society of the United States
2100 L Street NW
Washington, DC 20037
202-452-1100
www.hsus.org

Table of Contents

Foreword

By Ryan O'Meara

For as long as I can remember, I have wanted to work with dogs. Not just animals, but specifically dogs. I still, to this day, do not know why this overwhelming urge has stayed with me. My family did not have dogs while

I was growing up. But for some reason, from my early school days to late, I knew that my destiny lay in a career with dogs.

It's hard to put into words the intangible reward a person gets from a career working with animals. There are so many emotional pay offs, so many highs, so many indescribable joys. It's little surprise that working with animals is one of the most sought after career paths named by youngsters when asked what they would like to do when they grow up.

But to have a career with animals you need far more than just the desire. You need a plan too! How to Open & Operate a Financially Successful Pet Sitting Business is just the tool you need to set your plan into motion and to start a career doing what you love. With this book, you will learn everything you need to know about the business side of pet sitting. You will gain valuable information on start-up costs, writing your own business plan, and basic accounting and bookkeeping procedures. The CD-ROM included with the book is an invaluable tool for all new entrepreneurs. It contains all forms from the book and a customizable business plan for your own personal use, saving you time and frustration.

With pet sitting, you will need to know not only how to take care of the animals, but also how to serve your clients– the pet owners. With this book, you will learn customer service techniques that keep the customer returning again and again. Author Angela Williams Duea gives practical tips on ways to attract new business and advertise you services. She also suggests ways for you to expand your business by offering a variety of other services, such as pet walking, training, nutrition, and photography. How to Open & Operate a Financially Successful Pet Sitting Business includes everything you need to know so that you can confidently launch your new career and concentrate on the more important aspects of the job – the animals!

This book is an excellent resource for helping readers marry their passion and enthusiasm for working with animals together with the sound businesses principles and practical advice required to run a successful, professional pet sitting enterprise. Good luck with your business endeavors and happy sitting!

Ryan O'Meara
K9 Media Ltd
Box 9279
Mansfield
Notts, UK
NG20 0WU
Tel: 08700 114 115
Fax: 0700 608 87 24

Ryan O'Meara is a canine expert and editor-in-chief of the leading lifestyle magazine for dog lovers, K9 Magazine. *He also assists people in achieving their dream pet-related careers, with the animal career resource* ***www.WorkWithAnimals.com****. He is a successful author and media commentator on dog-related issues and is the founder of National Dog Adoption Month, helping thousands of shelter dogs find new homes.*

"There is no psychiatrist in the world like a puppy licking your face."
~Ben Williams

Introduction

A Nation of Animal Lovers

Americans are pet-loving people who have learned that caring for pets offers satisfaction, companionship, and fun. Pets lower blood pressure, ease loneliness, and help increase exercise. According to pet-owner surveys conducted by the American Animal Hospital Association, 94 percent of pet owners believe their pets have human traits and emotions such as curiosity, happiness, and friendliness. Over half of surveyed pet owners said they include their pets in family portraits, and 39 percent have given their pets a human name. Clearly, pets are beloved members of families.

You cannot always take your furry or finned family members with you when you travel. While kennels may offer humane, clean, well-cared-for facilities with lots of interaction, some animals are nervous or frightened in these facilities. Animals can become bewildered when they are dropped off at a strange location and their owners leave, and some pets have difficulty adjusting to a strange environment and routine while the masters are on vacation. Animals may have to be sedated just to get them to the facility. Pets may come home with colds, injuries, or fleas.

Case Study: Teresa Lewis

Teresa Lewis, Helping Hand Animal Care

Chesapeake, Virginia

In-home animal care is beneficial for both pets and their owners. Animals do much better in their normal, safe, and secure environment while surrounded by familiar sights, sounds, and smells. They will receive love and personal attention, and are able to stick to their normal routine while eliminating the trauma of an unfamiliar environment and exposure to other animals.

Owners will benefit by knowing their beloved pet is in the loving and caring hands of an experienced caretaker who can deal with any issue that may arise. They will also have a greater sense of security for their home with someone going in and out a few times a day.

Helping Hand Animal Care prides itself in offering more than the best possible care for animals. We take out the trash/recyclables, bring in the mail and newspapers, turn different lights on when we leave and adjust blinds and curtains. We can also water plants, scoop the yard and clean the litter box. If a client is not out of town but needs a dog walked, a horse lunged, or medication administered, we can take care of that as well. We tailor our services to the client and the pet's needs.

Why Pet Sitting?

Pet sitting can be a kinder and less disruptive option. An experienced professional who loves animals can care for animals in familiar surroundings and can cater to the pets' usual routine. When an animal is kept in a home where the sights, sounds, and smells are familiar, the pet will adjust much more easily to the family's absence. The pet is cared for by one person each day, and that sitter's focus remains on only those animals, rather than a kennel full of yapping pets.

The pet sitter provides the owner with peace of mind and a sense of security. If a water pipe bursts in the house, the sitter will be able to alert the family or a plumber — minimizing the damage that can be caused by a vacation's worth of water pouring into the home. The sitter can open curtains or blinds and randomly turn on lights giving the impression that someone is home. By picking up mail or newspapers, the sitter is removing clues that burglars look for in an empty home.

When I was a child, a neighbor would take care of our pets while we were away, and we often took our dog with us on trips. Today, people travel more often for business and pleasure than ever before, and in this mobile society people often do not even know their neighbors well enough to ask them to take care of their pets. Frequent pet sitting favors can put a strain on the goodwill of neighbors. In addition, no one wants to spend his or her vacation wondering if the neighbor child remembered to feed the dog every day or whether he or she brought over a bunch of friends to mess around in your house. What will happen if he or she cannot handle your big St. Bernard?

Even if you trust and rely on your neighbors, a bonded, insured professional can provide greater peace of mind. Pet sitters may have extensive experience in handling and caring for animals and may know basic first aid and medical care for pets. The bonding and insurance they carry lets the owners know that they are covered for accidental damage, theft, and personal injury. This peace of mind may help make a professional pet sitter a smart choice to take care of your animal friends.

Join a Growing Industry

Pet sitting has become a big business in the last 20 years. As a service industry, it has grown along with other types of services. The U.S. Department of Labor states that 96 percent of the job growth in the next five years will be in the service industry sector. Today's life styles may include service professionals who wash your cars, clean your clothes, mow your lawns, or cook your dinners (or deliver your pizzas), so that you are free for other activities. Americans are busy people, and service specialists increase your quality of life. With the attention and care lavished upon pets, people are more willing to hire someone to care for their pets as well.

America's pet-loving society spends 54 percent more money on pet food, toys, and care than three years ago. Pet owners report buying their furry "children" presents for Christmas, Hanukkah, Easter, and celebrating their animals' birthdays. The American Pet Products Manufacturers Association found that over 69 million households in the United States own one or more pets — a huge client base.

Whether you are located in a city, town, or on a farm, there are sitting opportunities all around you. Sitters in an urban location have the benefit of numerous households in a concentrated location, though people may be limited in the types of pets they are allowed keep. In addition, city dwellers often are disconnected from neighbors, so they may not have someone to rely on to care for their pets. People often move to suburban areas for yards and free space so that their children and pets have room to roam. The opportunity in suburban areas is that they are more family-oriented — and families love to adopt pets. On the downside, you may have to work a little harder to show clients the benefits of hiring you rather than a friend or the teenager down the street. In rural areas, you may have opportunities to care for farm animals like horses, cows, goats, sheep, chickens, and more domestic pets. Farmers with animals may be unable to leave home due to the animals in their care — and you can provide a welcome break. Servicing pets in the country may require more specialized skills and more driving.

A Rewarding Profession

Pet sitting is a unique field in which you are greeted every day by clients who are wriggling and dancing with excitement to see you. Your charges delight in the care you give them, from tossing a ball around a yard to sitting quietly while they are stroked. Their owners are relaxed and full of the assurance that their "babies" are given love and attention just as if they were home, and they know the pet is in comfortable surroundings. For a true animal lover, spending time with pets and caring for them can be more fun than work.

Besides the appreciation of your clients, pet sitting is a field in which there are no fancy, uncomfortable clothes to wear (or worse, uniforms); you are better off wearing tennis shoes, and the animals do not care what you are wearing. In the pet sitting business, you have control and flexibility with your own schedule. This is not a job with bankers' hours; you may do much of the work in the mornings and evenings, while the middle of your day is free. If you have a doctor's appointment, for example, you can schedule your daily visits around that time, rather than taking a few hours off work. If you need a gallon of milk, you pick it up on the way to your next call.

People may dream of owning their own businesses. Being your own boss, making decisions for yourself, and setting your own hours have an appeal that has led people out of corporate jobs and into their own offices. The pet sitting business is an ideal venture to start from your home, because little start-up money is needed, and you do not need to open a store or stock it with equipment or products. While the pet sitting industry has been predominately female to this point, men and women can find satisfaction and self-assurance in running their own business and nurturing animals. As a part-time job, sitting offers you additional income and the chance to spend more time with animals. Pet sitting is an ideal second career or retirement job, getting you out of the house and allowing you to keep being productive.

Let Us Get Started

This book is designed to walk you through each step of the starting and maintaining a pet sitting business. There is something in this book for all skill levels. For someone brand new to the field, this book will teach you all you need to know about becoming a business owner, about caring for pets, and managing their owners. Those of you who already have experience in sitting may find new tips and ideas by reading through each chapter, or you may want to jump to specific topics listed in the Table of Contents.

This book begins with basic information about business ownership and covers legal issues, business management skills, marketing, and animal handling. This complete manual will provide everything you need to know, including how to choose a name, getting started, pet sitting skills and tasks, handling exotic and farm animals, selling your services, billing and contract procedures, employee management, tax and computer skills, market research, promotional techniques, and expanding your business.

The companion CD-ROM will provide you with Microsoft Word™ samples of all the documents covered in the book. Business forms, contracts, time-management sheets, checklists, planning sheets, and other valuable, timesaving tools that no pet sitting business should do without are included.

Throughout the manual, you will find interviews and case studies from top professionals in the pet sitting business. They will share with you their perspectives on different aspects of the business and will provide tips to get your business running smoothly. These experts from across the United States are eager to teach new professionals their skills and want to encourage you as you begin your new career.

Now, let us get started!

1

About the Pet Sitting Profession

Would You Make a Good Pet Sitter?

There are several key characteristics of pet sitters that you must possess to be successful as a pet sitter. Before you open your own business, it is wise to assess yourself on these traits to be sure you have the skills you need. Some of these skills can be learned, or you can hire someone to fill in the gaps. Others are critical for you to have as the business owner. The following pages will help you consider whether you have what it takes to run your own pet sitting business.

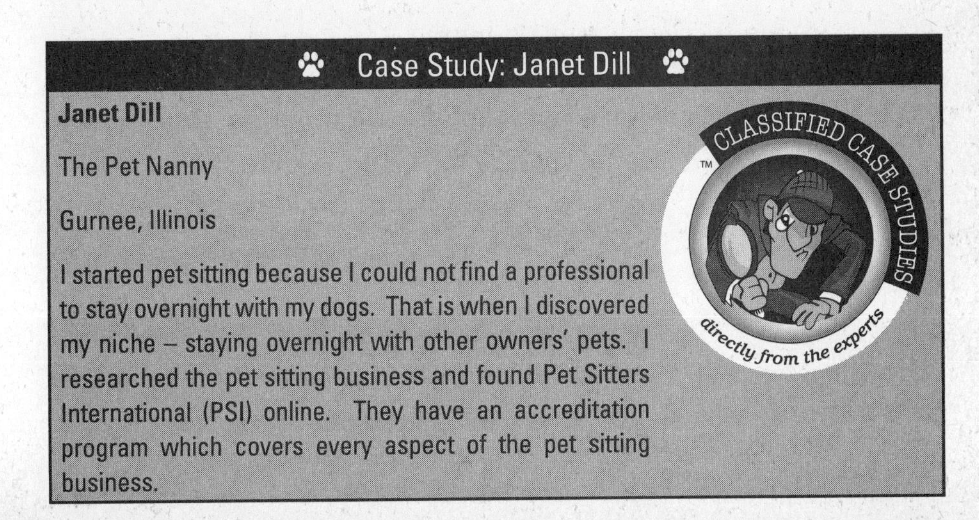

Case Study: Janet Dill

Janet Dill

The Pet Nanny

Gurnee, Illinois

I started pet sitting because I could not find a professional to stay overnight with my dogs. That is when I discovered my niche – staying overnight with other owners' pets. I researched the pet sitting business and found Pet Sitters International (PSI) online. They have an accreditation program which covers every aspect of the pet sitting business.

Case Study: Janet Dill

One must truly enjoy the types of pets they will care for. The sitter must also have a keen knowledge of the types of animals they sit for, to include behaviors and first aid. The sitter must be reliable, informed and have a good business practices plan.

To be a good pet sitter you have to not just like animals. You have to love them. If you do not find genuine pleasure in petting, playing with, and nurturing animals, pet sitting is not the business for you. You will spend plenty of your time around these creatures; you need to be sure you are a true pet lover. You should have a knack for reading animal body language — their nonverbal communication. Understanding the animals' nonverbals will enhance your ability to properly care for the pets. Pet sitting is about more than just playing with kittens. Even if you enjoy being around animals, taking care of pets will try your patience, your creativity, and your back muscles!

Ask yourself:

- Are you the kind of person who does not mind if you are covered in cat hair, or if a dog has left muddy footprints on you?
- Does a romp in the yard with a pet refresh you?
- Are you able to read an animal's signs when he or she is hungry, anxious, friendly, playful, or hurt?
- When you visit friends with pets, do their animals tend to gravitate to you?
- Are you comfortable with cleaning up animals' messes?

People think they would make a good pet sitter because they would rather deal with animals than with people. But the pet is not hiring you — the owner is. Your people skills must be every bit as good as your animal skills. If you cannot deal with humans, you will not be able to attract as many clients. A pet-crazy owner wants to find a sitter who will care for Fluffy the way he or she does, and the pet owner needs to feel a sense of rapport with you.

Case Study: Miranda Murdock

Miranda Murdock

My Pet's Buddy

Greenwood, Louisiana

The three most important pet sitting qualities are self-discipline, good judgment, and trustworthiness. The self-discipline is so important because you just cannot spontaneously "take off" if you are having a bad day. Many people think this industry is good for the flexibility. That is only partly true. It is flexible in so far as you can decide just how busy you want to be, but after you have accepted a job, then it becomes a little rigid — the pet's care depends on it.

Good judgment is necessary because you are left on your own to make many decisions as unexpected things happen — pets become ill, the heat in a home breaks down, or the dog or cat's personality changes when their owners are not around. You have to be able to make a sound decision and be able to back up that decision later.

The trustworthiness is self-explanatory. People are giving you unescorted, unsupervised access to their homes. They have to be able to trust you. Pet sitting is still considered almost a luxury service — responsible pet owners pay a good deal of money to have the peace of mind that their animals are receiving the best care possible. I want them to know that they do not have to waste a single minute of their vacation time worrying about what is going on in their home.

People skills not only help you find new clients, but they also help you deal with those clients. Clients can be frustrating, over-demanding, or push your limits. As in any profession, people are people. You will find some wonderful people who can become lifelong friends, and you will meet people who rub you the wrong way. Without firm boundaries, it can be easy to start out walking Fido three times each day and end up doing his family's laundry, and dishes, and taking out the garbage! You will need to deal with your clients with confidence and assertiveness.

Ask yourself:

- Can you conduct a professional interview with a stranger?
- Are you able to develop rapport with most reasonable people?
- Are you comfortable with enforcing payment rates and policies?
- Can you discontinue a financially or professionally unproductive relationship?

It is critical that a pet sitter be reliable and trustworthy. You are taking care of live animals that cannot take care of their needs themselves. If you do not feel like showing up for work one day, those animals suffer. It is critical that you do what you say you are going to do, and that you do it conscientiously. In addition, pet sitting is a unique business that has you working in someone else's home while he or she is not there. You must project confidence to the owners so that they feel comfortable with you being there. In everything you do, you should give them reason to trust you.

Pet sitters must always be dependable and self-sufficient. You will most likely perform your job on your own rather than bringing someone with you. you must be able to handle emergencies calmly and wisely without getting rattled. Think of yourself as not just someone to pour the food and brush the dog, but rather someone who is protecting the life of a family member and watching over his or her home.

Ask yourself:

- Are you able to make good decisions in difficult situations?
- Are you confident in working alone in a strange house?

- Can you care for a wounded, sick, or enraged animal without panicking or getting squeamish?

To own a pet sitting business, you must possess or develop good business skills. Every small business owner must manage the finances, advertising and marketing, employees, and administration of their business. It is crucial for you to maintain an excellent record-keeping process so that you do not lose track of who you are visiting Thursday afternoon or which pet receives an antibiotic with their dinner. Good organizational skills are necessary to keep on top of the many visits you schedule. You do not want to overbook yourself or forget a visit. If you appear unorganized in your paperwork or business practices, your clients could question if it is wise for them to leave a key to their home with you or whether they can count on you to care for their pets.

Owning a pet sitting business puts new demands on your business skills, and if you have not managed a business before the task can be daunting. However, business skills are learnable skills, not innate traits. It is hard to train someone who does not like animals to care for them, but you can learn to be an efficient business manager even if you do not like math. There are excellent resources for learning time management, administration, and business skills. After you have read this book, if you feel that you need help in learning to run a business, contact the resources at the end to build the skills you lack.

What is the final trait of a successful pet sitter? Good health. You must be able to keep up with animals, lift a reasonable amount of weight, and be able to walk and play with the pets. You should be in good enough shape that you can pull a cat from underneath a bed to give it a pill, or to pull a dog away from another dog that is getting too friendly. Whether you are sick or not, the pets need you, and whether there is an ice storm or a heat wave, you have to complete your appointed rounds. Make sure you maintain a healthy constitution.

If you answered yes to the self-assessment questions, you are ready to become a first-class pet sitter. If you are not sure of your skills, try spending some time volunteering at an animal shelter or working at a pet-grooming salon. While the fields are not exactly the same, you will get a taste of daily working with animals in a variety of situations. This should help you determine whether you would like to devote your energies to pets, or whether you would prefer to try another field.

Case Study: Terri Randall

Terri Randall

Creature Comforts Pet Care

Sheridan, Wyoming

My veterinarian suggested I become a pet sitter. I was in corporate America for a number of years when they pulled the proverbial rug out from under me by downsizing. I did not know it at the time but it was the best thing that ever happened to me.

I was feeling down and at loose ends and was at my veterinarian's office with one of my dogs for a routine exam. As I was telling him of my employment status he broached the subject of pet care. He said he had read an article about pet sitting and thought of me when he read it. He said "Terri, if the rest of my clients took as good of care of their pets as you do, my job would be considerably easier and more enjoyable. You were born to work with pets."

He was right. My entire life has always been full of pets of all kinds and revolved around them. I researched pet sitting for the next six to eight months and the rest is history. I started pet sitting April 1, 2000 and cannot imagine doing anything else.

I am certified in pet first aid and CPR. I have a number of special needs pets such as diabetics that need injections. I am educated and comfortable in handling these special pets. I am also currently working on my certification in canine massage and will offer that after becoming fully certified. I offer overnight care under special circumstances (meaning I stay in the client's home with their pets) and pet taxi services for pets for their vet or groomer appointments.

A Day in the Life of a Pet Sitter

Throughout the course of one day, a pet sitter might be an accountant, an animal care specialist, a groomer, a security guard, a marketing genius, and an office manager. Though each day varies in its activities and responsibilities, a description of a sample day should give you a clear expectation of your new career.

If you have a full day of appointments, the day will begin early. You will pack your car with your service kit (described in Chapter 5), daily schedule, your clients' keys, and directions. The night before you would have planned your day and determined the most efficient route for your visits. The time you spend traveling is time you cannot spend on an appointment, and the gas you waste on an inefficient route will cut into your company's profits.

A pet visit (detailed in Chapter 5) usually takes between 30 minutes and an hour, depending on the care requested and the number of animals. With each visit, you will provide food, water, and exercise to the pets, check their health, and clean up any messes. If you have agreed to any additional services, you will perform those now, and check the house for security and safety. At the end of each visit, you will want to record a comment for the client about their pets, a nice customer service touch that will help them feel connected to their companions while they are gone. You could have multiple visits to the same house during one day. At the end of your schedule of visits, you should double check your agreements to be sure that no animal has been overlooked.

During the day, you will also meet with potential clients. This interview allows you to meet the pets and owners, discuss expectations, and fully describe your services. This is a time for you to explain your credentials and experience. If you decide to take the job and the client is interested in hiring you, you will want to have him or her show you the house and indicate where the food, toys, and any other supplies necessary for pet care are kept. For more information on client interviews, see Chapter 7.

An important part of each day will be record-keeping and accounting. These tasks are described in the next few chapters on setting up an office and maintaining operating procedures. Taking care of these tasks on a daily basis will ensure that nothing is overlooked and the work does not pile up. Each day you should file your client and pet information, record information about visits, and write down your mileage. If you have employees, you will record their time information and you will also manage their paychecks. You will need to deposit payments, record expenditures, and enter them in your ledger. Each day you should spend time planning the next day, and looking ahead. Keep on top of your paperwork and stay organized so that you are not overwhelmed.

This general schedule gives an idea about the daily life of a pet sitter. A business owner will have to work on advertising the business, developing new clients, and monthly financial tasks. Each of these activities is necessary to build a successful business for yourself.

 Case Study: Miranda Murdock

Miranda Murdock

My Pet's Buddy

Greenwood, Louisiana

I retired from the military after almost 28 years of service. At that time my sons were older; the youngest was 11 and the oldest was 16. It was difficult to not work. I went to work part-time for the police department. After two years with the police department, I started to get the itch to run my own business. I thought about child care, but the huge liability issues involved with that were unsettling to me. I did not want to put our assets and our retirement at stake.

I have always been comfortable with animals, and they are comfortable with me — the family is always amazed by it — I thought that would give me a solid foundation. The start up costs were reasonable, and I did things myself to keep them even lower. Being retired, I had the time to thoroughly research the industry before making the jump, and I was not dependent on the income for my livelihood during the start-up phase — the "waiting for the phone to ring" time.

Typical Pet sitting Services

The following list shows the most common services that pet sitters offer. Chapter 10 will encourage you to look beyond these services to new methods of expanding your business.

1. **Drop-in Service**: A sitter goes to the pet owner's home for one, two, or three visits per day. Average visits last 30 minutes for cat sits or 45 minutes for dog sits. This is the most commonly offered service.

2. **Daily Dog Walking**: A sitter provides walking services for pet owners that work long hours or when dogs are locked inside. An average walk is 20 minutes in the middle of the day. Puppies, which will not be able to last a day without going outside, can also benefit from a romp midday.

3. **Picking up pet supplies/Errands**: A sitter picks up food, litter, and medications. This is a less common service, but if you are asked to do it, make sure you charge for your time and mileage.

4. **Transportation to Vet or Groomers**: A sitter drives a client's pet to an appointment. This is less common because of time and liability during transport.

5. **Grooming**: A sitter bathes a dog with shampoo and towels provided by owner. If the dog needs special grooming the owner already has a professional groomer doing it. During the course of a sitting visit the animal could need extra grooming — especially if he or she has rolled in the mud or made a mess in the house.

6. **In-home Boarding**: The pet stays in the sitter's home. If you are performing this service while also performing drop-in sitting

appointments, think carefully about whether this arrangement will work for you. You will not be at home to watch the pet, and he or she could try to escape. Pets can be destructive to your home by clawing or urinating on your furniture. Most communities only allow a certain number of pets in your home before you have to be licensed as a kennel. Check with your local zoning laws before offering this service.

7. **Overnight Service**: A sitter stays in the home from the evening hours until the next morning for a 12-hour period, such as 7 p.m. to 7 a.m.

8. **House Sitting**: A sitter stays in the home the entire time — a full 24 hours. This is less commonly offered because the sitter cannot take on any other jobs, making it a less profitable arrangement.

The Animal Population of the United States

From dogs to horses to ferrets, 63 percent of all American households care for some sort of pet. The National Pet Owner Survey of 2004 found that pets outnumber humans by 100 million in the United States. With all these animals, only about one million people currently use the services of a pet sitter. Your market is 63 million customers!

Cats are the most commonly owned animal, with dogs placing a close second. There are plenty of fish, bird, and reptile lovers as well. The following table shows the populations of many common animals, as of 2005, determined by American Pet Products Association.

Americans own:

- 91 million cats
- 74 million dogs

- 17 million birds
- 11 million reptiles
- 10 million saltwater fish
- 139 million freshwater fish
- 18 million small mammals (guinea pigs, gerbils, mice, and chinchilla)

Other pets and farmyard animals not included in the survey, are:

- Horses
- Goats and sheep
- Ducks and chicken
- Cows
- Rabbits
- Monkeys
- Potbellied pigs
- Tarantulas
- Sugar Gliders
- Bush babies
- Wallabies
- Llamas and Alpacas
- Hedgehogs

Some sitters specialize in wildlife recovery, which has special regulations by state.

Consider the list. Which pets do you already have experience with? Are there any animals you would like to learn more about? Do you know of any animals that you absolutely would not handle? Do you think you might handle a gecko, but never a crocodile? Could you feed a boa constrictor its favorite dinner — a mouse? These are important questions to shape your learning path and to determine the services you will offer. Note that farm animals and exotics require specialized knowledge. This means you might have to do more work up front to learn about them, but you might be able to charge more for customized or unusual services.

Gaining Credentials and Experience

You have spent some time thinking about your traits and animal experiences — an important step. Owners want to know you are qualified to care for their pets and that you have relevant experience. You must be able to show your customers that you know how to feed, groom, and care for their animals, and that you have some basic first aid and health information about the breed.

Case Study: Stephanie Erway

Stephanie Erway

Furr Pet's Sake, Inc.

Denver, Colorado

CLASSIFIED CASE STUDIES™
directly from the experts

Get experiences handling animals. Ask your local veterinarian if you can volunteer your time. Some veterinarians will allow you to shadow one of their technicians. If you do not have pets, volunteer your time at the local humane society.

Pick up books on animal behavior or visit with your local behaviorists and learn as much as you can about animals, such as what it means when their tail is down between their legs and other signals that animals give. Get a dog and take it to an obedience training class.

One way to gain and prove experience is by having pets of your own. Pet owners gravitate to pet owners, and knowing how to care for your particular species well is the best way to learn how to care for other peoples' animals. If you do not have animals of your own, you certainly do not need to advertise the fact. There are other ways to gain experience in pet care. You can work for a veterinarian or pet groomer or interview him or her on his or her skills and ask the them to teach you information you need to know to care for and groom animals on your appointments. You can take care of pets for friends and neighbors. Perhaps you might volunteer at a homeless animal shelter or help out at animal shows or training facilities. Contact a pet food salesperson to ask if you can follow him or her on the job for a day — and gain valuable information about pet nutrition. Check with your local colleges and farm bureau offices and enroll in any applicable courses or seminars on animal care, equine studies, or similar appropriate offerings. Each of these opportunities will provide you with references and on-the-job experience, and those references tell potential clients that other people think you are reliable, trustworthy, and talented.

For those who have pets of their own, completing dog obedience classes or nutritional seminars can be an asset to your business. You can showcase your skills by working with a client's dog to teach it to behave. If he or she has been pestered by Lassie jumping up on him or her as a greeting gesture, your client could be impressed to see that you can train her to sit. You might even consider adding obedience training as an extra service, for which you charge more. Imagine your client's pleasure when he or she comes home from a vacation to find you have broken his or her dog of a bad habit!

Licenses and other credentials can be helpful. By joining your local Chamber of Commerce you lend business credence to your new company, and you make valuable business and professional contacts. While a membership will not persuade a client to hire your services, you are indicating to potential customers that you are a business professional, which will add trustworthiness to your sitting service. The Better Business Bureau is another organization that can help give your company visibility. This organization maintains high quality standards for its members, including a lack of complaints, truthful advertising, objective descriptions of products and services, and honest disclosure of charges. Businesses who abide by these standards can be considered trustworthy, honest, and reliable — all traits you should project in your business.

Membership in professional pet organizations is another method to provide credentials and project a professional presence. You will find organizations specifically related to your field, devoted to a particular species or breed, or focusing on special activities such as breeding or grooming. Each membership you maintain will show clients that you are a respected name in the pet culture and that you maintain professional ties. Local organizations will help you develop a network of friends and business partners and potential clients. Nationwide organizations, such as Pet Sitters International, will connect you to a vast network of resources, support, and education. Check online sources and your yellow pages for listings on these organizations.

Pet Sitters International (PSI) offers pet sitters an accreditation program to sharpen their professional skills. An in-depth educational program teaches pet sitters about pet care, health and nutrition, business management, office procedures, and additional services. The top pet sitting professionals in the industry have worked together to develop this coursework.

While you can gain this knowledge in other places, such as by reading this book, PSI offers accreditation for students completing this coursework. Your clients will know that by hiring an accredited sitter, they are assured of hiring a professional with in-depth knowledge and skills in caring for pets and a good knowledge of modern pet-care practices. To become accredited, the pet sitter has to learn and exhibit a working knowledge of taking care of many types of animals and running an efficient business.

Pet Sitters International maintains a quality standard for those in the pet sitting business. Clients can feel secure and confident with their choice of sitters when a company upholds the following quality standards.

- The company is bonded and insured.
- The sitter provides references.
- The sitter visits the client's home before the first pet sitting assignment to meet the pets and get detailed information about their care.

- The sitter shows a positive attitude during the initial meeting and seems comfortable and competent in dealing with animals.
- The company provides written literature describing services and stating fees.
- The sitter is courteous, interested, and well-informed.
- The sitter wants to learn as much as possible about the animals in his or her care.
- The sitter has experience in caring for pets and is clearly mindful of their safety and well-being.
- The company and sitter exhibit courtesy and professionalism in all dealings with staff, customers, and industry colleagues, presenting the pet sitter and the pet sitting industry positively.
- The company keeps regular office hours, and answers client inquiries and complaints promptly.
- The company has a veterinarian on call for emergency service.
- The company has a contingency plan for pet care due to inclement weather or personal illness.
- The company conducts business with honesty and integrity, and observes all federal, state, and local laws pertaining to business operations and animal care.
- The sitter takes precautions to make sure a client's absence from home is not detected due to any careless actions or disclosures by the sitter.

- The sitter calls to confirm or has the client call to confirm that the client has returned home.
- The company provides initial and ongoing training for its pet sitters.
- The company refrains from criticizing competitors.
- The company provides a service-rating form for clients.
- The company carefully screens applicants for employment.

A tool you will find valuable over the years is the Merck Veterinary Manual. Merck is a highly-regarded company in the field of animal care, and this book offers a wealth of reliable information on animal health and care. There is plenty of general information about most species of animals you will encounter as a pet sitter and more technical information for those who would like to expand their skills and knowledge.

This book can be found in bookstores, ordered directly from Merck, or purchased from online stores such as Amazon.com. The manual is also searchable online at **www.merckvetmanual.com**. If you prefer, you can order the manual as a CD-ROM; you could load this onto a laptop that you take with you for reference while you are keeping pet sitting appointments. The information you learn about animal care will enhance your ability to give the best-quality care to pets.

An accurate assessment of your abilities and strengths will give you confidence that you have placed yourself in the right career. Identifying your areas of growth will help you plan for your educational needs and help you find learning resources. As you plan for the types of animals you will care for, you will gain confidence in your new profession. After you have a clear understanding of the demands and needs of this profession and have begun to build some credentials and professional references, you are ready to take the next step: setting up your business for success.

Case Study: Stephanie Erway

Stephanie Erway

Furr Pet's Sake, Inc.

Denver, Colorado

I was working for a veterinarian as a veterinary technician, and I was asked on several occasions to take care of sick animals. I decided I liked dealing with animals that were not close to death's door. I made some business cards and a brochure and started handing them out to local veterinarians and people I met that were walking dogs.

I plastered them on cars at the local pet store. I gained interest in my business through extra services I offer, such as nutritional counseling, pet parties and medical treatment that the veterinarian has already approved to be done at home. I am able to give subcutaneous fluids, administer injections and change bandages.

"Animals are such agreeable friends - they ask no questions, they pass no criticisms."

~George Eliot

Home Business Basics

A small business owner is a jack-of-all-trades. You must be the financial planner, manager, accountant, president, and play a host of other roles. Starting a home business involves putting in hard work, taking other people's advice, and a dealing with a steep learning curve for a new owner. You will need to choose the right business structure, select a name for your business, estimate costs, create a business plan and budget, manage financial accounts, and set rates and services. This chapter will guide you through these tasks.

Choosing Attorneys, Banks, & Accountants

There are professionals who can help you design your business for success and keep you on track. Finding a good bank, business attorney, accountant, and tax advisor can help you significantly. To find the right team of professionals, ask friends and other business owners who they use. A yellow pages search may turn up good candidates, as will a call to the local bar association or professional organizations.

An attorney will help you ensure that your business complies with all the legal and licensing requirements that small businesses are subject to. In the following sections, I recommend that you obtain advice from a lawyer when choosing your business structure, trademarking your business name, and setting up a corporation, if necessary. You will want a lawyer's advice when you write a basic pet sitting contract that you will offer to clients, if you hire employees, and if you apply for a business loan.

While you may find that one consultation with a lawyer will take care of all your questions and needs, you might find it helpful to cultivate an ongoing relationship with an attorney in case further issues or needs arise. For this reason, it is important to find a lawyer you can work with long-term. If you find during your initial consultation that you do not feel comfortable with him or her, try another lawyer. Their first consultation, even over the phone, may be free. The right lawyer for you will be one who is interested in your business plans and engaged in making them become a reality. An energetic and enthusiastic lawyer will expend energy on your behalf. Make sure your attorney is knowledgeable about small business legal issues, preferably someone who specializes in the field.

A good accountant can help you with complex financial accounting and give you guidance on managing your financial affairs. Your business will require you to keep good records, and if you hire additional employees, an accountant can take care of your payroll. It is important to find an accountant you feel comfortable with, and who will maintain a long-term relationship with your business. The right accountant will be willing to initially set up your books and then train you on how to maintain accounting procedures. He or she will also make your job easier by supplying tax forms and planning tools, and advising you on year-end tax matters.

When you are choosing the bank that will handle your business, select the bank based on convenient hours of operation, bank account features, local branches, low fees, and customer service. Once you are busy making sitting calls, you do not want to be stuck with a bank that does not offer easy depositing procedures or is never open at a time convenient for you. Make sure you understand their policies and procedures and where to find supplies in the bank when you are setting up your business. You may be too busy later on to take time for these tasks.

There are several specific services you may need for your business. You must set up a business checking account separate from you personal checking and savings accounts to keep your accounting simpler. You may want a business debit or credit card for company purchases. If the bank offers a merchant credit card, you will be able to accept Visa and MasterCard payments from clients.

When I first set up my business, I considered all these options, but I also considered another factor: personal service. I wanted a team of professionals I could count on to give me the best advice and products, and I wanted real people that wanted to work with me, rather than a faceless organization. Though large institutions like national banks can offer much in the way of additional perks and services, I wanted personal attention and the chance to help out another small business.

With this in mind, once I found an attorney I felt comfortable with, I asked him if he had any suggestions on an accountant. If he was giving his mom advice, where would he send her? The lawyer recommended an excellent, service-oriented accountant. When I was exploring banks, I found a local bank where the tellers call me by name and recognize me when I stop by. Once, when the bank manager was reviewing reports, he saw some suspicious activity on my account and called me to help me straighten out the problem. These are truly members of my business team.

Your Business Structure

When you start your own business, one of the first things to consider is the business structure you will use. The legal structure of your business will determine such things as how you will manage your tax obligations, whether or not you will have partners, how you can sell or transfer your business to another party, what decisions you are authorized to make for your business, and how you can be legally held liable for the business. Types of business structures include sole proprietorships, partnerships, corporations, and legal liability companies. It is important that you understand each of these companies so that you set up your business according to your needs.

A **sole proprietorship** is most commonly used for small businesses with few assets and a single decision-maker; many pet sitting businesses are set up this way. Having sole proprietorship means that you are the business. This type of business cannot be transferred or passed to another person; if you die, the business ceases operation and will pass to your estate. You have total authority and control, and unless you hire employees, you do not need to apply for a federal employer identification number. Your identification number is your Social Security number. The business itself does not pay the taxes; you will record your profits and losses on your personal income taxes. You fund your business through your own assets and credit sources.

People choose the sole proprietorship option because it is the easiest and cheapest to set up. There are some business and filing fees, but fewer legal restrictions. Your business licenses from state and local authorities may be the only setup activities you need.

The disadvantages to a sole proprietorship are also the reasons why it is attractive. Because you are the company, you assume unlimited liability for the business in the event of damages, lawsuits, financial problems, or business losses. All your personal assets (home, bank accounts, and autos) can be seized to pay out losses. While unlimited personal liability can sound frightening, the new pet sitting business owner can protect him or herself against such risks by obtaining sound legal advice, saving enough capital to cover financial losses, and obtaining sufficient insurance to cover potential problems. Later in this chapter, insurance coverage will be addressed.

A **partnership** is similar to a sole proprietorship, but the business is owned by two or more people. This makes sense if a husband-and-wife team or two or more friends build a sitting business together. The partners share decision-making authority, control, responsibility for profits and losses, and liability. Each partner is considered an agent for the business who is liable for the actions and debts of the other(s). A partnership can be as simple as a verbal agreement, but a formal agreement drawn up by an attorney is a better choice.

A business attorney can handle setting up an agreement that will define the responsibilities and boundaries of the partnership. It is critical to have an agreement in place before problems or disagreements occur between partners. Even best friends can have differences of opinion about how to run the business. An agreement should define the amount that each partner has invested in the business, the way that the partners will share profits and losses, how each partner will be compensated, how the assets would be distributed if the business partnership dissolves, the duration of the partnership, how they will handle disputes, and what restrictions will be placed on authority and spending. If new partners are added, a new agreement must be drawn up.

Partnerships are easy to set up, but they do require partners to apply for business licenses and a federal identification number. While partners will record profits or losses on their individual tax returns, they will also file federal and state forms indicating the partners' profits and losses.

The advantage of a partnership is that it increases the resources you have to work with to build your business. A partner may provide more capital to start the business, another source of knowledge for the business, and an extra pair of hands to complete the work of setting up your company and attracting clients. Having a partner in a pet sitting business means you have a backup to help with clients or take over when you are not available. A good partner will make your job easier.

A **corporation** is a legal entity separate from a person. Corporations are complex entities that cost more to set in place than the other business structures. A corporation is chartered to do business by the state in which it is located. Rather than a single person or partners who own the business, a corporation is owned by stockholders who have raised capital by buying shares in the business, and whoever has the greatest number of shares has the most control over the business. The owners then receive profits from the corporation in the form of dividends. The stockholders elect a board of directors who oversees the business and protects the stockholders' interest in the business.

Because a corporation is a separate entity from a person, the corporation does not end if you die, and the business can be transferred to another person. The major advantage of a corporation is that it limits an individual's liability in the business. The corporation itself is responsible for its debts and losses. The stockholders may lose their investment if the business is unprofitable, and the directors may lose their position if they have made bad business decisions, but in most cases these people will not put their personal assets at stake for the corporation.

Despite these advantages, setting up a corporate business structure is costly and time-consuming. The owners must apply for corporate status, write bylaws, and submit articles of incorporation to the state agency that charters corporations, issues capital stock, and records ownership. The record keeping and filing fees can cost the business owner several hundred dollars. On an ongoing basis, business decisions must be well-documented and formally filed. The owners must hold an annual stockholders' meeting and elect directors and officers each year. When filing taxes, the corporation must pay income taxes on its profits, and the stockholders pay income taxes on their dividends. While a corporation is an entity that can be scaled up from small- to mid- or large-sized businesses, the requirements may be more complicated than a new business owner desires.

There are several variations on a straight corporation. An **S corporation** is a distinct type of structure that offers a business owner limited liability and some tax advantages. While it must comply with the legal requirements of regular corporations, the profits pass through to the stockholders according to the amount of stock they own. Though the S corporation files tax returns, they do not pay any corporate income tax. **Limited Liability Companies** (LLCs) and **Limited Liability Partnerships** (LLPs) are two other newer legal structures. They offer similar liability protection and pass the profits through to the stockholders, but they offer an easier setup process than a regular corporation. A business lawyer can provide direction with these types of structures.

Naming a Business

Though naming your business might seem like the easiest part of starting your own business, there are several key things for you to consider. The name of your business will be with you for a long time. Take it seriously. Choose several and ask family and friends for their opinions. Is your name right for you? Is it catchy? Do you want to include your full name in the business or register an assumed business name?

Your business name should be easy to remember and describe what you do. For example, your pet-owning clients may not immediately think of hiring you to sit their pets if your business is called "Paws and Wings," but "Pet Sitting Professionals" will indicate your work and your expert status. A name that is difficult to pronounce will make it more difficult for your business to spread by word of mouth. While a pun or rhyming name can be memorable, be careful not to get too cute with the name. You want people to see you as a professional.

Make sure that the name you are considering is not already in use, or does not sound similar to another business name. If another corporation already uses that name, you will not be able to use it, and you do not want people to mix up your business and hire the other guys instead of you. The United States Patent and Trademark Office (PTO) or a business attorney can inform you on whether another business has already registered your business name; if not, obtain the PTO forms and trademark your business name. If you do not, and another company registers it for itself, you will be legally required to change your name. This action will compel you to print new stationery, business cards, and brochures. You will also have the undesirable result of confusing your clients and potential market.

If you have chosen to use your complete name in the business, such as "Jane Doe's Pet sitting Company," you will not need to register your name with your local city hall or town clerk's office. But if you have chosen a title that only includes part of your name, like "Jane's Pet Sitters," you will need to register the fact that you are doing business under another name (labeled "d/b/a"). While this does not protect or trademark your name, it does allow the public to know who owns your business. Fees for this registration vary from state to state, but your city hall will have the information you need to register.

Case Study: Christi Marks

Christi Marks

All Tails Pet Care

Green Bay, Wisconsin

CLASSIFIED CASE STUDIES™ directly from the experts

To pick my name and start publicizing my business, I just tossed around names for a couple weeks. I made sure to look online and in the yellow pages. If something sounded good to me, I made sure there wasn't something else like it. I am at the top of search engines and listings as the business name starts with an A.

I first put out some flyers and listed my web site and phone number on many search engines online. I put an ad in the yellow pages. Word-of-mouth is huge in this business. You start with friends and it branches out quickly. Just get your name out there, walk in a hometown parade with a banner and hand out business cards, and put up flyers. The Internet is a huge help; everyone is looking online for everything.

Creating a Business Plan

A business plan is crucial to your new business because it will help organize your business efficiently from the start. If you are looking for capital to run your business, lending institution decision makers will want to see your plan before they agree to invest money in your business. If you want to attract partners, you must be able to show them you have a well-thought plan for your business.

Business planning sounds dull, especially when you would rather be taking care of pets, but it can be fun. A business plan should contain several important sections: a summary, an industry overview, your credentials, an operating overview, and a financial plan. Below, the structure of the business plan has been outlined for you.

1. Executive Summary
    - Objectives
    - Mission Statements
    - Keys to Success

2. Company and Management Summary
    - Company Ownership
        - Startup Summary
        - Startup Funding — Financing Options
    - Management Summary
        - Personnel Need Projections
        - Personnel Plan

3. Products and Services
    - Product and Service Descriptions
    - Sales Literature
    - Technology
    - Future Products and Services

4. Competitive Analysis
    - Competitive Analysis in a 20-mile Radius

5. Facility Accreditation
   - Interior
   - Exterior

6. Certification of Employees
   - Manager
   - Kennel or Day Care Attendants

7. Target Market Analysis Summary
   - Target Market Segment Strategy
   - Market Needs
   - Market Growth
   - Service Business Analysis
   - Business Participants

8. Strategy and Service Implementation Summary
   - Competitive Edge
   - Marketing Strategy
   - Pricing Strategy
   - Promotional Strategy

9. Sales Forecasting
   - Industry Occupancy Percentages
   - Establishing Pricing Positions

10. Financial Planning
    - Startup Expense Analysis
    - Key Financial Indicators
    - Break-even Analysis
    - Projected Profit and Loss
    - Projected Cash Flow
    - Projected Balance Sheet

Though these terms may sound a little intimidating, writing out the business plan is not a daunting task.

First, write down a summary of what your business is and what it will offer. This summary will also be used as a 60-second personal commercial when someone asks you what you do. Be creative and descriptive. Not everyone has heard of pet sitting as a business, and you have the opportunity to introduce people to the industry while you may even attract a client.

Next, write down an overview of the pet sitting industry, especially any animal specialties that you expect to target for work. This section is important because you will mine these areas for work, and you will continually evaluate to see if you are expending effort in the right direction. This book can be a resource for defining the industry, especially with statistics on the number of pets per household, how often pet owners use pet-care professionals, and the amount spent on pet care products in the United States There are many online resources, such as Pet Sitters International's web site, that can help you describe this. You should review the listings in your local yellow pages under "Pet Sitting," "Pet Care," and "Animal Care," and talk to veterinarians and groomers to see how much competition already exists in your field. If the competition is considerable, brainstorm ways to make your business different or more attractive, and include that information in the Strategy and Service Implementation section of your plan.

Next, write down your credentials, which is where the business plan becomes fun. You get to list all your accomplishments and strengths — do not be afraid to brag about awards, training, and experience. List any previous jobs that gave you experience in pet care. Make sure you use active, interesting descriptions of your work and note any special accomplishments, such as managing others or increasing profits. If you are a little weak in any of these areas, you do not need to point that out, but work on gaining credentials using the tips in Chapter 1. Then include your training and credentialing plan, with specific dates and milestones, in the Company Survey section.

Write out a description of how you will operate your business. In this Company Summary section, you will describe where your office is located, what types of security you have in place (you are maintaining sensitive information and the keys to peoples' homes), whether you will have any employees or partners, and what supplies you will need to set up your office and run the business.

Finally, write a financial analysis of one-, three-, and five-year earnings. This will help you show investors and partners your strategy, help you estimate your income, and plan for the future. Later in this chapter you will learn how to set rates for your services. You will use that information to determine your monthly and annual profits, income, and expenses. It is realistic to assume that your first year will be a ramp-up period, and then your income goals can become steadier after that point. If you plan to start part-time, your ramp-up year may cause you little to no financial pain. Pet sitting is the perfect part-time job because with little equipment and good abilities, you can begin your business with a flexible schedule.

Pull all this information together and keep it in a safe place. On a monthly basis, check back with your plan to see if you are on the right track. Your business plan might change, or your course may need to be corrected. With a detailed plan, you can keep your business focused.

Case Study: Christi Marks

Christi Marks

All Tails Pet Care

Green Bay, Wisconsin

CLASSIFIED CASE STUDIES™ directly from the experts

I was raised around all sorts of pets. We had horses, cats, rabbits, goats, birds, and dogs. My parents showed English Setters for many years when I was growing up. Animals are a pure love of mine. I started looking into pet sitting after my fiancé and I bought a house and got a dog of our own.

I started to look more closely at what options people have for their pets when traveling or working long hours. As for many people, our dog Milly is our baby; we want only the best for her. It seemed to me allowing families to leave their pets at home in the best of care while they were gone was a no-brainer. That's when I got serious and looked into web sites, insurance, pet sitting forms, and all I needed to start my own business.

Case Study: Christi Marks

The most rewarding part of my profession is having happy pets meet me at the door. It is fun when they get your routine down and know exactly who you are and what you will be doing each day. It is such a joy. Keeping these pets happy is so fulfilling.

Setting Rates and Services

In the previous chapter you were asked to consider which animals you are willing and capable of caring for and if there are any pets that you would avoid. Next, you need to consider what services you are willing to offer.

Pet sitting experts agree that the basic pet sitting appointment takes about 30 to 60 minutes including driving time. During that basic visit a sitter will exercise or walk the pets, check their health, feed them, bring in any mail or newspapers, and water plants. The sitter will check the house for obvious signs of entry or danger, change the position of drapes or blinds, or perhaps switch on different lights so that the house appears occupied. Some sitters offer additional services such as grooming, brushing, or bathing. Some sitters offer to stay overnight with the animals. Another sitter might water or mow lawns or take care of the garden while the owners are gone. Adding on a trip to the vet or an obedience lesson will allow you to add on extra charges to the bill.

After you set a basic rate for an appointment, consider how you will handle additional animals. Many clients you meet may have more than one pet in the house, and your fee schedule should take this into account. Clients may ask you to care for other pets for free. Some pets, such as cats, may take just a little time to care for, and they may argue that it only takes a few minutes to check on a hamster and give it some food and water. However, this is time that you could spend on another appointment with a client who is paying you full price. Do not sell your time cheaply. You may want to add a small charge ($2 to $5 per visit or per day) for easy-care animals like cats that will entertain and exercise themselves, or a flat fee for each additional pet. If you are caring for farm animals, such as a flock of sheep or chickens, you would charge per visit, not per animal, since the cleaning, feeding, and watering will be only done once.

Finally, consider whether you will charge more for holiday visits. Some sitters charge more since they are taking time away from their own families; they consider it a common business practice to charge more for premium times (akin to a plumber who charges more on nights and weekends). Other sitters consider that their clients are most likely to use sitting services during holidays, and thus a base rate is reasonable.

To set the rate for basic services, you will need to consider your cost to provide service. The cost of your service call goes beyond the gas you use to get to the appointment. It includes all the costs of your business:

- Licenses
- Professional fees
- Rent and utilities (for an office outside the home)
- Supplies
- Marketing materials and costs
- Employee, payroll, and benefit costs
- Automobile expenses
- Insurance fees

If these costs add up to $500 per month and you are able to make five visits each day for 30 days, then your cost per visit is $3.33.

To determine how much profit you expect to make, you should consider the value of your time. If you could be working as a bank teller for $12 an hour, your profit opportunity is $12 an hour. Thus, for an hour-long pet sitting visit you could reasonably charge about $15, which includes about $3 in cost and your $12 opportunity.

You need to determine what people are willing to pay. You can check with other pet sitters in your area or do some research with pet sitting organizations. Consider whether your area has an average cost of living or is higher/lower than the average; urban areas tend to be higher, and rural areas tend to be lower. This is important information to help adjust your rates against a national average. People will pay according to the "utility" of your service: the satisfaction, peace of mind, or value a client perceives in your service. For example, you can compare your services to the peace of mind a client gets after he or she obtains quality day care for a child. The client knows that the child is happy, well-cared-for, and safe; he or she is willing to pay a child care professional $10 to $20 an hour for care. Many clients love their pets like family members; a rate in the $10 to $20 range is not unreasonable.

Once you have determined a base rate, you can then add to it for special services. Extra items, such as grooming or longer walks, might be charged according to your hourly rate. For example, if you charge $15 a visit for a half-hour appointment but also walk the dog an additional 15 minutes, you can charge an extra $8 for the 15-minute walk. In determining the basic rate, you plan a 30-minute visit and 30 minutes of travel time. If it takes longer to get to and from your client's house than 15 minutes, you may want to charge extra for the visit. An easy way to do this is to define a service zone for your work. Your basic zone might be ten miles or less from your home. A client who is ten to 20 miles from home might be an expanded service zone for which you charge extra — perhaps mileage reimbursement (number of miles x current government rate of 40.5¢ a mile) or an additional $5 per visit. Finally, you will need to obtain a key from the client before the first visit, and you will want to consider whether you will absorb the cost of the travel or whether you will charge a fee for retrieval and drop-off of keys.

There are two other considerations on setting fees: whether the fees are too high or low and whether you have specific income needs that must be met. If you have a specific income need not met by your planned rate structure, you will need to determine whether you will work longer hours, cut costs, or charge more to meet your goals. If you set your fees too low, you may attract more customers, but your profit may be too small to be sustainable. If you set your fees too high, your clients may not see enough value to want to hire you — or may not want to contact you a second time.

You can always re-evaluate rates once you are established or when you have new credentials or services. When you change rates, though, you will have to re-publish any materials that showed your original rates. You may have difficulty with current clients who are satisfied and comfortable with current charges, but who may be unwilling to pay the increased rate.

Once you have set your rates, it is a good business practice to stick to them. You may run into trouble if you give a friend a discounted rate and then he or she quotes that rate to people he or she has referred to you. You should treat all your clients fairly. At other times, though, you may sit for a client that requires little traveling (such as a neighbor across the street), and you may feel uncomfortable including a travel cost in his or her rate. Some visits may take substantially more effort than you originally estimated, and you may need to re-negotiate. To give yourself some room to negotiate, you might consider quoting a new client a range of prices, rather than a set rate.

When you have a specific rate structure defined, you must think about how you wish to handle payment. Some sitters require full payment in advance while others ask for a deposit and then receive the balance after the work is complete. You will want to consider whether you will charge the client for a missed interview or a cancellation. While that may sound a little harsh, during busy times you may be booked and need to turn away requests for appointments. If someone cancels his or her appointments at the last minute, you are losing money unless you can fill those hours. This is a standard business practice among many professionals such as doctors and lawyers who charge by the appointment, and you are every bit the professional they are.

Estimating Startup Costs

The start-up costs for a pet sitting business are not substantial. You may be able to set up your business with a few thousand dollars, including fees for business licenses and attorney costs. The most important investment in your business is reliable transportation. You will spend much of your pet sitting day on the road, and you cannot afford to have your car break down. You cannot afford to use a car that gets poor gas mileage or you will eat up your profits at the gas pump.

The following checklist will help you estimate what you will need to start up your business. These items are the customary needs for a pet sitting business; you may think of some additional items, or you may remove items you do not need or already have. This form is included in your companion CD-ROM.

- ☐ Business License(s) Name Registration
  - ☐ Local
  - ☐ State
  - ☐ Federal
- ☐ Attorney Fees

- ☐ Business Name Consultation and Registration
- ☐ Legal Structure Costs (Partnership Agreement, and Incorporation)
- ☐ Business Form Development and Review Accountant Fees

☐ Insurance

- ☐ Liability Insurance
- ☐ Dishonesty Bond
- ☐ Disability Income Insurance
- ☐ Automobile Umbrella Coverage

☐ Office Expenses

- ☐ Deposit for Office Space
- ☐ Rent for Office Space
- ☐ Moving Expenses for Office Site Setup

☐ Bank Charges

☐ Telephone Expenses

- ☐ Business Telephone Deposit
- ☐ Business Telephone Installation
- ☐ Monthly Charge for Business Telephone (Purchase or Rental)
- ☐ Answering Machine and/or Personal Answering Service
- ☐ Cell Phone and/or Pager

- ☐ Monthly Cell Phone Calling Plan
- ☐ Monthly Internet Connection, Fee Calculator

☐ Office Expenses and Supplies

- ☐ Computer
- ☐ Software
- ☐ Office Furniture: Desk, Chair, Cabinet, Shelf, or Bookcase
- ☐ Business Form Printing, Business Form Purchase
- ☐ Basic Office Supplies
- ☐ Pet sitting Supplies
- ☐ Office, Library Books and Videos

☐ Advertising

- ☐ Web Site Design, Monthly Hosting
- ☐ Local Publications, Newspaper, Yellow Pages, Other
- ☐ Television, Radio

☐ Professional Affiliations and Subscriptions

- ☐ Annual Dues for Pet Sitters International, Chamber of Commerce, Pet-Related Organizations, Better Business Bureau
- ☐ Reference Books, Business-Related, Pet-Related, Other
- ☐ Magazine Subscriptions, Business-Related, Pet-Related, Other
- ☐ Convention Registration and Travel Miscellaneous

Insurance and Bonding

Liability insurance is important to your business, though there is no legal requirement to obtain this coverage. Insurance will protect your business assets if anyone ever claims damages or losses because of your business. Animals are unpredictable, and anything can happen in someone else's home. You want to be protected if you accidentally knock over a valuable vase or if the dog injures itself in the yard under your watch.

In the early years of the pet sitting industry, insurance agents were not as familiar with the profession as they are now. While the concept of pet sitting has become more widely accepted, your insurance company may not have a ready-made policy for your business. You may have to work with the company to design a policy that covers your needs. Your general liability policy should cover accidental damage and personal injury, and "care, custody, and control" coverage. Pet Sitters International also provides a Pet Sitters Liability Protection Policy written specifically for our industry.

It is important to have good coverage on your automobile, since you will be doing a fair amount of driving. Check with your insurance agent to see whether you will benefit from an additional rider in case you are in an accident while pet sitting. If other employees will be driving your car to appointments, make sure your coverage is adequate.

A Dishonesty Bond or Surety Bond protects your business and your clients in the event of a theft. The bond should pay the client the amount of any theft, and then the bonding company recoups the payment from the convicted pet sitter. If you are a trustworthy person with no employees, you may only want to purchase a bond of several thousand dollars as a good faith gesture. If you are covering other employees, purchase an amount that will help you sleep well at night, knowing that you will not have to reimburse a theft if one of your employees turns out to be dishonest.

Business Accounting

There are a few terms that you need to understand to manage your business accounting system. While your accountant may have referred to these terms and procedures, he or she may not have given you a clear understanding of the meaning. These basic business accounting principles will guide you through managing your finances.

Managing Your Accounts Receivable

If you plan to offer credit, it's important to track what you are owed on a monthly basis. You should know how much of your account is in extended credit to customers, and view how that credit is aging so you're aware of overdue payments. A receivables aging report looks like the following table:

	Total	Current	30 Days	60 Days	90 Days	Over 90 Days
Accounts Receivable Aging						

Make a plan for how you will deal with slow-paying customers.

- When will you call the customer?
- When will you escalate to sending a formal letter?
- When will you get a lawyer involved?

Managing Your Accounts Payable

When your business owes money to other businesses, it is call an Accounts Payable (AP). You should keep track of what you owe to others and how long you have owed it in an AP aging report, so you can plan who to pay and when it should be paid. If you pay before it is due, you will deplete your cash, but if you pay late, you may have to pay extra in late fees or interest If you know you will be late with a payment, be sure to notify the creditor.

A payables aging looks like the following table:

	Total	Current	30 Days	60 Days	90 Days	Over 90 Days
Accounts Payable Aging						

Debits and Credits

Your General Ledger (GL) is where you keep track of all your business accounting. The core of your GL is the debits and credits you account for. Each accounting entry in the general ledger contains both a debit and a credit – money coming in and money going out. Obviously, the amount of all debits must equal the amount of all credits, or your account is not balanced. In fact, many software accounting packages will check the debits against credits and notify you if there is an imbalance.

The type of account will determine whether a debit or credit will either increase or decrease the account balance. For example, when you are accounting for income, a debit will decrease the account while a credit increases the account. On the other hand, when you are accounting for your expenses, a debit increases the account (you now have more expenses) while a credit decreases the account (you now have less expenses).

Each time there is an increase in one account, there is an opposite (and equal) decrease in another. For example, if you have a new expense entered in your expense account, this means that you have a decrease in your income account.

Account	Type Debit	Type Credit
Assets	Increases	Decreases
Liabilities	Decreases	Increases
Income	Decreases	Increases
Expenses	Increases	Decreases

For every increase in one account, there is an opposite (and equal) decrease in another. This keeps the entry in balance. Debits always go on the left and credits go on the right.

Look at these two sample entries and try out these debits and credits. First, suppose that you have finished a long sitting job with a client who now owes you $1,000. Your accounts read:

Accounts Receivable	$1,000
Sales Income	$1,00

If you looked at the general ledger right now, you would see that receivables had a balance of $1,000, and income had a balance of $1,000.

Now suppose you have just collected a payment from the client:

Cash	$1,000
Accounts Receivable	$1,000

Notice how both parts of each entry balance — the receivables balance is back to zero. That is as it should be once the balance is paid following the normal time between the recording of the receivable and its collection.

Accounting does not get much harder. Everything else is just a variation on the same theme. Make sure you understand debits and credits and how they increase and decrease each type of account.

Assets and Liabilities

Balance sheet accounts are the assets and liabilities. When you set up your chart of accounts, there will be separate sections and numbering schemes for the assets and liabilities that make up the balance sheet.

A quick reminder: Increase assets with a debit and decrease them with a credit. Increase liabilities with a credit, and decrease them with a debit.

Identifying Assets

Assets are things of value that your company owns. The cash in your bank account is an asset. So is the company car you drive. Assets are the objects, rights and claims owned by, and having value for, the firm. Since your company has a right to the future collection of money, accounts receivable are a major asset.

Identifying Liabilities

Liabilities are the opposite of assets. Liabilities are amounts that you owe to another company. In your accounting system, your Accounts Payable are liabilities, because they are amounts that you must pay to another company in the future. For example, if you order a quantity of flea collars and dog shampoo, and are required to pay your bill at the end of next month, you have a liability that must be paid next month.

Owners' Equity

After the liability section in both the chart of accounts and the balance sheet comes owners' equity. This is the difference between assets and liabilities.

Your main goal is to have positive: assets exceed liabilities, leading to a positive owners' equity. At the end of one accounting year, all the income and expense accounts are netted against one another, and a single number (profit or loss for the year) is moved into what is called the retained earnings account. This is what belongs to the company's owners. That is why it is in the owners' equity section. The income and expense accounts go to zero. This is how we are able to begin the new year with a clean slate.

The balance sheet, on the other hand, does not get zeroed out at year-end. The balance of each asset, liability, and owners' equity account rolls into the next year. The ending balance of one year becomes the beginning balance of the next.

Think of the balance sheet as today's snapshot of the assets and liabilities that your pet-sitting business has acquired since the first day of business. The income statement, in contrast, is a summation of the income and expenses from the first day of this accounting period (from the beginning of this fiscal year).

Balance Sheet

The balance sheet, on the other hand, does not get zeroed out at year-end. The balance of each asset, liability, and owners' equity account rolls into the next year. The ending balance of one year becomes the beginning balance of the next.

Think of the balance sheet as today's snapshot of the assets and liabilities that your pet sitting business has acquired since the first day of business. The income statement, in contrast, is a summation of the income and expenses from the first day of this accounting period (from the beginning of this fiscal year).

Income and Expenses

Further down in the chart of accounts (usually after the owners' equity section) comes the income and expense accounts. Most companies want to keep track of just where they get income and where it goes, and these accounts provide that information.

A final reminder: For income accounts, use credits to increase them and debits to decrease them. For expense accounts, use debits to increase them and credits to decrease them.

Expense Accounts

Most companies track a separate account for each expense type so they can analyze their expenses and track them over time. It's likely that you will have the same type of expenses each month, so once you've established each account, the accounts will not change much from month to month. Typical pet sitting expense accounts include:

- Salaries and wages
- Telephone
- Utilities
- Fees
- Promotional materials/services
- Rent
- Automotive (insurance, maintenance, gas)

Once you have mastered basic accounting principles, you will be able to run your business like a professional. The next chapter guides you through setting up your home office.

Setting Up an Office

After you have licensed your business and set up your business structure, you will need to set up an efficient, well-stocked office with procedures in place to lead your business to success. This chapter focuses on the equipment, supplies, and processes you need to manage your work.

First consider the location of your office. While many pet sitters plan to work from home, some prefer to rent space or buy an office building. Make sure your area is zoned for business before setting up an office in your home. There are tax and life style advantages to having a home-based business, but check with a tax advisor to be sure this is still advantageous to you.

If you want to set up your business in your home, there are factors to consider. While it can be enjoyable to have no commute and to be in close proximity to your office, people who maintain home offices may have problems. Their families may not respect their office time, they may work longer hours because the work is in the home, or they may be distracted by daily household tasks when they should be focused on business. Think of your office as a separate work space with specific hours, and you will not shortchange your family or your business.

Be sure you will have the discipline to work from home without becoming sidetracked or too focused on work. Be sure you set up boundaries with your family. I work from a spare bedroom solely dedicated to my business. When the door is shut, my family knows that I must not be disturbed except in extreme emergencies. There is a whiteboard and a bulletin board on the door so that people can leave me notes or affix something to the door that needs my attention when I am available. This has worked well in our household.

If you will be working with a partner or other employees, consider whether they will be comfortable working out of your home and whether your family will be bothered by strangers coming in and out of their house. You should also be sure that you will be able to maintain a professional environment, especially if you have small children who might get noisy while you are in the middle of a business call.

Equipment and Supplies

If an office outside the home is a better option for you, choose a location central to your service area. An office does not need to be luxurious; you can choose bare-bones accommodations to reduce your overhead costs. Whether your office is in the home or in a separate facility, the equipment you will need is the same:

- Table or desk
- Chair(s)
- Shelving for supplies
- Phone (a cell phone is best, but you will need a business phone)
- Answering machine or service
- City/area maps

- Calculator
- Computer, word processor, or typewriter
- Locking file cabinet

Not everyone has a computer or typewriter. Though computer programs can make your job simpler, they are not necessary for your business. You can perform accounting on paper forms and hire a typist to make contracts and client forms for you. If you are not comfortable with technology, these options may make your life easier.

If you do want to use a computer, there are many software programs that will help you manage your business. Microsoft® Money and Intuit® QuickBooks are two programs that can help you manage your business accounting; these systems are user-friendly, easy to learn, and inexpensive. There are also several software programs to help sitters save time and effort by consolidating scheduling, sitter and client communication, invoicing, payroll, and client/pet information. EZ Pet-Sitter, Professional Pet Sitter, and Pet Professional software are common; information can be found on each system through their Web sites. If you like the convenience of technology, these types of programs are worth the investment.

In addition to equipment for your office, you will also need supplies. These supplies include:

- **Schedule book, calendar, or personal digital assistant (PDA)** This will help you keep track of appointments and sitting visits. It is crucial to keep good notes about your time commitments to ensure an animal is not missed or that you are not overbooked.
- **First-aid supplies for humans and pets.** You may want to put together a traveling first-aid kit to keep with you on appointments.

- **Reference books or videos on pet care and animal breeds.** It is important for you to keep yourself current with information on breeds, animal care, and trends in your profession.

- **Stationery and envelopes with your business name, address, and logo.** Choose a style and color scheme that you will use throughout all your marketing materials, and your business will become a recognizable brand.

- **Business cards.** Professionally printed cards are inexpensive, but they will convey a professional image to your clients.

- **Printer paper.** You will need this is you choose to use a computer and printer.

- **Brochures or flyers about your business.** Professionally-printed materials will leave an impression with potential clients.

- **Notepads.** These are helpful for leaving notes for your clients and for phone messages.

- **An accounting ledger and accounting forms.** If you will not be using a computer program for your finances, you will need these for your paperwork.

- **Business forms.** Contract and client information forms will be essential tools for you.

You will also need basic office supplies like pens, scissors, tape, postage stamps, labels for folders and house keys, paper clips, a stapler, file folders, and correction fluid. You can certainly use any supplies you already have around your house, but if you buy supplies for your business, be sure to keep each receipt. You must be able to account for all expenses you claim on your tax return.

You may want a city or area map for your office. You can hang it on the wall and quickly see whether a new client is in your service area, and what route is most convenient between visits.

Sitting Supply Kit

Before you go on your first pet sitting appointment, you will want to put together a bag of things to take with you. Resist the urge to pack in everything you could possibly use on an appointment; the bag will be too big to carry. Pet owners have all the common items you will need to care for their animals. Be sure your bag always contains the items you will need to complete the day's appointments and pack it the night before so that you are not running around in the morning and forgetting something.

In your sitting supply kit, you will pack your daily schedule, the next day's service contracts, extra business cards, flyers, and pens. Carry a supply of self-addressed, stamped envelopes to leave at your clients' house for payment. A clipboard to hold service contracts will be helpful to your clients when they are filling out your forms. You will need a key ring or key holder of some kind to carry your client's keys. If you choose a bracelet band or a ring that clips onto a belt, you will save yourself the trouble of accidentally locking the key in the house, or of having the wind knock the door shut while you are in the yard with a pet. Make sure you pack city maps for your service area. A flashlight is a good idea to pack for a visit to a dark house or for a pet hiding under a bed. You may want to bring an extra leash in case you cannot find the pet's leash or in case one breaks on a walk.

Finally, pack your first-aid kit, pet toys, a beverage, and your lunch or snacks for the day. Pet sitters sometimes spend the day on the run, and the temptation to hit a fast-food place for lunch can make your health suffer. If you will be going to questionable areas, check into regulations about carrying pepper spray or a squirt bottle of lemon juice or vinegar, and always keep some form of identification with you. These items could protect you.

Business Phone and Address

Your business should have a separate business phone line. Phone companies have policies about using business lines rather than personal lines for a company. You could incur penalties or fines by violating their policies. In addition, with a business line your company can be listed as a business in the yellow pages of your phone directory rather than in the residential listing. If a potential client is looking for your business name in the directory, it will be hard for them to find you by your personal name. Finally, by having a separate line for your business, you can handle business calls during business hours and more easily walk away from your work at the end of the day. Calls to a personal line can be harder to put off until your business opens the next day. A business phone line is also considered a business expense when it is time to do your income tax return.

A cell phone is an important tool for a pet sitter if you can afford one. Since you will be on the road for much of each day, it is helpful to be accessible to your clients and have a means of communication. You will be going to people's homes alone. Consider how a cell phone will give you a measure of safety in unfamiliar areas. With a cell phone you are always within reach in case of emergencies or last-minute changes.

Whether you have a business line in your office or direct all business calls to your cell phone, it is important to handle calls with professionalism. Answer your phone politely with the full name of your business and your name: "Good afternoon, Jane Doe Pet sitting; this is Jane. May I help you?" Be sure you answer the phone promptly when you are available for calls. A missed call could mean a missed opportunity for new business. However, when you are engaged in a sitting appointment, focus on the animal, not your phone calls. Suppose you are talking with a potential client, and the dog you are walking slips out of her leash or picks a fight with the neighbor dog. Your potential client will hear the commotion and wonder how much attention you will give his or her pet.

Pet sitting is a service industry, and good customer service is important. Personalize your answering machine or voice mail message, and your clients will notice. Try saying, "Hello, you have reached Jane Doe's Pet Sitting Service. I am out taking care of furry friends right now, but I will be glad to respond when I return. Thanks for calling." If someone has left you a message, be sure to respond promptly. You want clients to know you are accessible and reliable.

When you are talking to prospective clients, allow your warm, friendly, pet-loving side to shine through in personal touches. Just saying, "You have an Irish setter for me to take care of? I love those dogs — my aunt had two of them when I was growing up," can give customers the sense that you are enthusiastic about animals. They will be more likely to hire you. Anytime you are on the phone, remember to smile. Your callers will not see your smile, but they will hear it in your voice.

Your business needs a business address, not your home address. If you have rented office space outside your home, you can use the office address. However, you may want to consider a post office box, whether your office is in your home or in another building. A post office box will protect your family's privacy when you work from your home. Unless you want someone to drop off a litter of kittens at your house or office in the middle of the night, you will want to protect your street address from the public. Post offices charge a small fee for post office boxes. After you receive a box address, put it on everything: your bank account, business cards, and yellow pages phone listing.

Internal Revenue Service Issues

Business owners pay separate taxes for the business. You will be taxed based on your business structure. There are several other taxes you will be expected to pay as an employer, such as Social Security and income taxes.

As an employer you are responsible for deducting income taxes from your own and your employees' pay. Small-business owners may make quarterly estimated tax payments to state and federal government when they expect to owe at least $1,000 in taxes for the year. Paying taxes on a quarterly basis is easier than paying the entire annual tax bill at once. An accountant can help you correctly calculate your taxes for each quarter.

As soon as you open a business, you are eligible to deduct many of the costs of running the business from your income tax return. The Internal Revenue Service (IRS) tax code provides direction on what expenses can be deducted, as follows:

> *Internal Revenue Code § 162.*
>
> *Trade or business expenses.'*
>
> *(a) In general. There shall be allowed as a deduction all the ordinary and necessary expenses paid or incurred during the taxable year in carrying on any trade or business, including:*
>
> > *(1) a reasonable allowance for salaries or other compensation for personal services actually rendered;*
> >
> > *(2) traveling expenses (including amounts expended for meals and lodging other than amounts which are lavish or extravagant under the circumstances) while away from home in the pursuit of a trade or business; and*

(3) rentals or other payments required to be made as a condition to the continued use or possession, for purposes of the trade or business, of property to which the taxpayer has not taken or is not taking title or in which he has no equity.

Pet sitters can deduct travel and food costs while on the road to pet sitting appointments. They can also deduct any other expenses related to running the business. While tax laws concerning home offices have become more strict, you can still claim the following types of expenses:

- **Depreciation on business furniture and equipment.** According to the IRS, you can depreciate furniture and equipment such as computers, desks, chairs, file cabinets, copiers, and fax machines, over five to seven years.

- **Depreciation on the portion of your home that is used for business purposes.** You can depreciate the business part of your home over 39 years. This deduction carries a cost since when the home is sold, business owners may owe taxes on any depreciation costs they have deducted. For that reason, analyze the pros and cons with your accountant.

- **Other real-estate expenses.** These include real-estate taxes and home mortgage interest. Just as they do with all expenses shared between the personal and business parts of a home, entrepreneurs are entitled to deduct the portion of those costs that relate to the business.

- **Strictly business expenses.** This category includes the costs of special business insurance policies (or the cost of amending a homeowner's policy), additional utilities, home business cleaning, and repairs on office equipment. Other home expenses that can be justified on a strictly business basis, such as the need to install a security system, also qualify for a full deduction.

If you sell retail products in your business, such as a line of pet care products or animal toys, you must pay state sales tax on these goods. Register with your state as a sales tax vendor and report your financial records on all the goods you sell on a monthly basis. Some states offer electronic filing, which saves time. On the Internet, the IRS maintains a helpful Web site that may answer questions for you. For all tax issues, be sure to consult with a tax attorney or accountant who is familiar with small business. This may save you time and trouble.

Handling Payments

There are a number of methods of accepting payment from your clients, from simple cash and check transactions to credit or debit cards and online payments through companies like PayPal. With so many options, it makes sense for a business owner to offer clients many ways to pay. There are some advantages and disadvantages to each payment method. Carefully consider the types of payments you will accept. For every form of payment, make sure the client receives a statement or receipt. Keep a detailed copy of the receipt for yourself.

Credit and debit cards offer flexibility, ease of use, and convenience to customers. These cards offer ways for your clients to pay over the phone or via a paper form. If you are able to accept credit and debit cards, you will save your clients time and will receive your payment faster. However, there are set-up costs and fees to business owners who accept these cards. Be sure a banking agreement has terms in your favor. To accept credit and debit cards, you will need to open a merchant account with a bank and have your credit reviewed before acceptance. Not all banks offer merchant accounts. Shop around. You will need an electronic data terminal or handheld credit card machine to read the card and record the card data.

PayPal is an online payment service that offers flexibility and convenience. The company is designed to transfer money from buyer to seller online through accounts that each party sets up. The money is removed directly from the buyer's checking, savings, or credit card account and deposited to any of those accounts that the seller owns. Accounts are secure and easy to set up at **www.paypal.com**. In a few mouse clicks, clients can send payments directly to your bank.

If you accept payment by cash, it is important to record the transaction carefully. Cash is harder to trace than any other form of payment; your receipt book is more important than ever. Give one copy of the receipt to your client while keeping one for yourself. If you have a number of clients who like to pay by cash, you will need to make more frequent stops at the bank to deposit your earnings, since carrying large amounts of cash is not a good idea.

Many people like the convenience and security of writing checks, but this can be the most troublesome form of payment for business owners. All other forms of payment are guaranteed to you, but a check can be written for money that is not available. Bounced checks can cause you frustration and extra work. Because it is a popular form of payment, consider what policies you need to put in place to deal with returned checks and fees.

Managing Your Time

When you work for another employer, your time is not your own; you must keep the hours he or she sets and work when you are told. When you work for yourself, setting your hours and planning your work schedule can be troublesome. Some people find the freedom to work from home and choose their work hours can be a temptation to do other things and become distracted; others find themselves working long hours and sacrificing family and leisure time. Each temptation requires self-discipline to make the home office work.

There is always something that can distract you from your business when you work for yourself. On a particularly nice day, you may prefer planting flowers in your garden or going for a long walk. Your children may run in and out of the office with papers for you to look at, friends to meet, or arguments to overrule. Stay-at-home friends can drop by or call for a lunch date. You have a dozen errands to do and there is a sale at the department store. Each of these distractions of daily life can derail your business. Plan carefully to handle these problems. Some people use daily calendars to block off work time, family time, and self time. Different colored ink can let people know at a glance which activity is your priority at that moment.

When I started my business, I realized that one of the major reasons I left a corporate job to work for myself was the ability to blend my work and home life. I wanted to be available for my children when they stepped off the school bus. I wanted to cultivate my friendships and take advantage of those beautiful spring days. That meant I had to set boundaries on when I could be disturbed during work hours. I told my family and friends when I was available for phone calls and shut the office door when I could not be disturbed. I shifted my hours to take advantage of school schedules and night-time hours when my husband was able to take care of the children . I developed the mind-set that if I was disciplined and worked hard during hours I set for myself, I would be able to take advantage of my flexible schedule and take an afternoon off once in a while.

Though you are working from home, it is important to set regular working hours. Otherwise it can be easy to distracted by throwing a load of laundry in the washer or fixing that wobbly ceiling fan. Once others know you are home, you might have to field calls from the school asking you to help the teachers each morning or run the food drive. Consider whether these activities will eat into your work time and whether you are willing to sacrifice your business for these activities. If you are not, just say "No," no matter how much you may want to help.

Dedicate yourself to work during your work hours, and when your work day is finished, close your file drawers and office door and be present for the other parts of your life. Do not take paperwork out while watching TV, or handle phone calls during family time. It is important to your health and your family's well-being to be present and focused, without living, breathing, and sleeping your new business.

Case Study: Christi Marks

Christi Marks

All Tails Pet Care

Green Bay, Wisconsin

Your pet sitting business is a huge demand on your time. You'll have early-morning visits, late-night visits, and appointments on weekends and holidays. Those are the busiest times: holidays and weekends. You have to be committed to the job, but the reward of getting to visit all these happy and grateful pets is well worth it.

I would not be able to do it without backup support. My mom, Sharon, and my husband, Trevor, are my "employees." They back me up and help out when I am not available or when I can't make all the pet sits on my own. They are a valuable asset to my business. Enlisting volunteers or paid employees would help any pet sitting business.

Business Do's and Don'ts

Do's

1. **Price your services appropriately.** Complete a survey of the pet sitting business already in your area to price your service. You can

find sitters in your area through your Yellow Pages. You should also do a search of pet sitters through the Pet Sitters International Web site **www.petsit.com**, or the National Association of Professional Pet Sitters at **www.petsitters.org**.

Call pet stores, veterinary hospitals, and groomers near your home and ask if they recommend any local pet sitting businesses. Go to local pet stores, vets, and groomers to see if they have any cards on display.

When you contact local sitters, say, "I am a new pet sitting business owner and I want to price my services appropriately. Would you mind telling me what you charge? Also, I would like to network with someone in my area to refer to when I am taking time off or am overbooked. Would you be willing to mail me a business card?"

2. **Network with other sitters.** Many sitters have reported that a significant number of their clients come from referrals from other pet sitting companies they have networked with or met through professional associations.

3. **Limit your area of coverage.** Start with no more than a ten-mile radius from your home and decrease that area as you have sufficient clients in a smaller radius. Your profit is dependent on how far you drive; the more you drive, the less you make.

4. **Determine your maximum number of appointments.** If you are a full-time sitter with all your appointments in a ten-mile radius of your home, the most appointments you should book in one day is 14 individual sits. However, if you did that many for long you would burn out. A full-time sitter may have ten visits during the busy season and four visits a day during the slow season.

5. **Avoid burnout.** This is a seven-day-a-week job. You do not have weekends or regular days off. Make sure you take time off, find a backup sitter, and network with others to provide support.

6. **Find another sitter to cover for you.** This is the best reason to network with other sitters in your area. You may have a personal emergency or need to take some time off; having a colleague cover for you is essential.

7. **Be patient with your business growth.** Most businesses take one to three years to generate full-time income.

Don'ts

1. **Do not price other sitters out of the market.** You may think that charging less than other sitters will drive customers to you, but this can be a big mistake. Pet owners may wonder why you are the cheapest service in town. You might also end up with clients other sitters do not want to take. This is not a high-paying job to begin with. If you price your services below market rate, you are setting a low value on your time and skills.

2. **Do not print too many forms and brochures.** These can be costly; you do not want to use up your entire startup budget on forms and flyers. Additionally, you may want to make corrections and additions to your information after you have been in business a while, and it may be harder to justify printing new promotional materials when you have a case of 5,000 still in your garage.

   It is illegal to put flyers in mail boxes without stamps, and it is inconsiderate to put flyers under car windshields in parking lots. Most people do not appreciate that and will likely throw them away.

3. **Do not take pet sit assignments anywhere other than your office.** You run the risk of losing information if you're recording it on the road. Keep your business records in your office.

4. **Do not overbook pet sits.** There are unethical sitters who overbook appointments in such numbers that they could not possibly care for all the animals each day. Instead, they visit the pets every other day or every third day of the job. This is considered fraud, and sitters who engage in this practice will ruin their business and reputation, and they will face fines and jail time (especially if an animal is endangered by their actions).

5. **Do not refer problem animals or clients.** If you have struggled with a non-paying client, a filthy home, or a dangerous animal, do not refer them to another sitter to get out of the job. This unethical behavior will ruin your reputation and could put another sitter in danger.

6. **Do not criticize other sitters or clients.** There are many ways to communicate and network, including Internet forums, associations, and industry message boards. Whatever you post on these boards is public information that anyone can read; your words will reflect positively or negatively on your business. Always be professional and gracious, and handle conflicts person-to-person.

Managing Personnel

As you build and expand your business you will need to consider whether to hire additional employees for your services. As a new business owner, you may conclude that managing other employees is an overwhelming task on top of the activities surrounding a new business. But when you decide to hire additional employees, you will have a number of things to consider.

First you will need to think about what you want your employees to do. Do you need an administrative assistant or an additional sitter? Do you want a part-time or full-time sitter? Or are you just looking for someone to handle overflow or emergency situations? Do you want an employee who will work for you or perhaps a subcontractor that provides his own insurance and works independently but carries a work contract with you?

Next, consider the type of person you want to hire. There are key characteristics of pet sitters that someone must possess to be a success. During the interview process described below, you will want to assess the traits that will show you whether or not the person is the right choice. You will need to determine whether or not you and the prospective employee will click. Will the person fit in with other employees? Is this someone you feel comfortable working with long-term?

Posting a Job Opening

You will find and hire the best employees by crafting and publicizing a strong job notice. There are several ways to advertise an open pet sitting position, depending on your budget and the number of people you want to attract. In most cases, posting an ad in local newspapers and carefully-selected Internet sites is the best way to begin advertising your position. You can also try placing recruiting posts on pet sitting Web sites and organizations. If you are looking to hire more than one employee for the same type of job, you might try recruiting at area pet events, veterinarians' offices, or colleges.

Be as specific as possible about your needs and the precise level of the open position. Try to make the job sound exciting while being realistic about what the potential employee can expect. Job postings are meant to draw a number of applicants, but they should also help you narrow the field of candidates. Writing a job posting gives you a better idea of who you are looking for and offers potential candidates a clue as to whether the position might be right for them.

After you have posted your job opening, be patient. Running one ad in the newspaper for one week may not be enough. Be realistic about the number of responses you might receive, and try to mix the mediums in which you advertise.

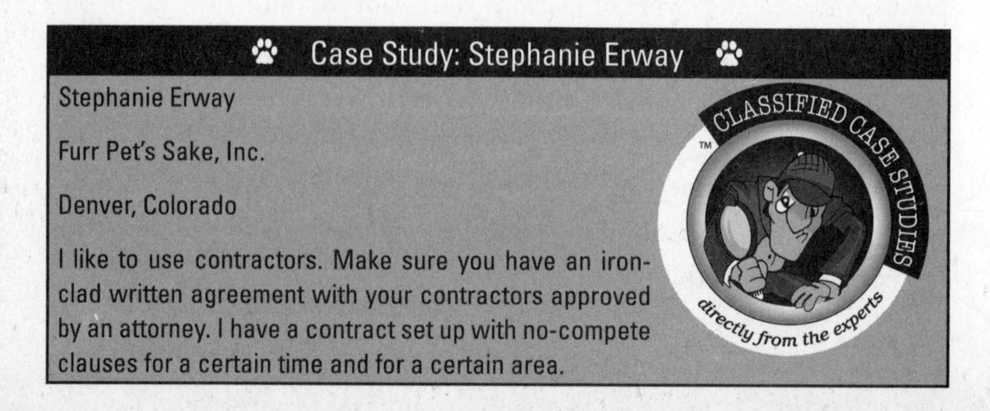

Case Study: Stephanie Erway

Stephanie Erway

Furr Pet's Sake, Inc.

Denver, Colorado

I like to use contractors. Make sure you have an iron-clad written agreement with your contractors approved by an attorney. I have a contract set up with no-compete clauses for a certain time and for a certain area.

Case Study: Stephanie Erway

It also states that if they were to leave, all materials, keys, and forms must be returned to the company; otherwise they will not receive their last paycheck. It is not foolproof, but if they know anything about contracts they will be less likely to try and take your clients from you.

Build a good working relationship with your sitters. Make sure you talk to them every day. Make sure they use invoices that you make up with a numbering system on them. I spend time with my sitters, and we have monthly meetings. I use a form that the client fills out after each sitting stint that allows the client to tell me how the sitter did. Clients sign a contract that gives them instructions on how payment is mad, and to confirm their visits with the office, but nothing is embezzlement-proof. If you have to prosecute, then do so. Then let your new sitters that come to work for you know that you mean business and are not afraid to have them arrested or taken to court.

I prefer to hire women in their late 40's and 50's who are married and looking for a part-time job. They tend to be people that do not need the money but just enjoy working with animals and want to get out and make some spending money.

Interviewing a Potential Sitter

There are different philosophies when it comes to the interview process. Some business owners look more closely at specific animal-handling skills; others will be concerned primarily with how an individual will fit into the business, and others will focus on an applicant's enthusiasm and desire for the position. The need to handle specific tasks, supervise others, meet with clients, and work independently will factor into how you approach the interview process and make your assessment of potential employees.

Although you can get answers to many questions by looking at a resume or job application, it is important to hear each prospective employee respond to questions. They provide greater insight into their previous employment and education.

The following questions are important starters:

- What did you do at your last position?

- What did you like about your last position?

- Why did you leave your last position? Or why do you wish to leave your current position?

- How would you describe your relationship with your coworkers? Supervisors? Clients or customers?

- What accomplishments are you most proud of?

- In which areas would you most like to improve?

- What are your strengths and weaknesses?

You will also want to find out about the candidate's reasons for entering the field and their future plans or goals. You will need to assess their specific skills and character traits to help you determine whether they have what it takes to care for animals according to your standards. The questions below provide an assessment for each candidate. Rather than just asking these questions, and having the candidate say "Yes" or "No", rephrase them so they tell you about an experience that displays that skill. For example, rather than asking if they have a knack for reading animal body language, instead ask, "Can you tell me about some experiences where you have had to read animal body language when caring for pets? What was the result?" Carefully note each answer to help you make a decision later.

- Does the pet sitter love animals? Do they enjoy petting, playing with, and nurturing animals?

- Do they have a knack for reading animal body language?

- Are they comfortable with cleaning up messes after animals?

- Does the person show signs of trustworthiness?
- Can he or she build rapport with humans?
- Can he or she firmly enforce payment rates and policies?
- Is the sitter reliable? Does he or she project confidence?
- Is he or she dependable and self-sufficient?
- Are they able to handle emergencies calmly and wisely?
- Can they make good decisions in difficult situations?
- Are they confident in working alone in a strange house?
- Can they care for a wounded, sick, or enraged animal?

Be sure to schedule time after the interview to look over your notes and form impressions of the interview. Pay attention to any warning signs, your gut feel, and first impressions. If someone appears a bit "off" in an interview or has an undesirable behavior at the first meeting, these behaviors will multiply on the job. If an applicant does not show up well-groomed and in attire appropriate to the business, you can be sure they will not look or behave professionally on the job. If they do not show you respect and develop rapport, it is likely they will not use these traits with a client either. You may want to conduct an interview while your own pets are present and see how the applicant interacts with them. Seeing their ability to connect with animals first-hand is the best interview technique of all.

Compensating Sitters

After you hire another employee, you will need to consider issues such as pay and benefits. You will need to decide whether you will set a flat pay rate for the sitter or split a commission with them. When you set your rates consider the overhead costs and the profit you want to make on the business. Be sure you are compensating the employee fairly for the work; it must benefit them to work for you and not the sitter across town. Though many sitters join the business because it is enjoyable work, they will not stay for long if the pay is not lucrative and competitive. Organizations such as the National Association of Pet Professionals (NAPPS) or Pet Sitters International (PSI) can offer advice about average employee rates.

The current minimum wage is a good place to start. Factor in the level of responsibility and time demands when setting the rate. Make sure the pay rate will bring in the quality of worker you want to represent your company. While some businesses pay by the hour, others pay by assignment or by a percentage of the total charges. For example, a new sitter might earn 40 percent of the total earnings for the job, while an experienced sitter working for you might command 60 percent of the total. The rest is earned by you as the manager, investor, and risk-taker in the business.

The Federal Small Business Administration provides the following information about employee payroll deductions:

> *Employers are responsible for withholding taxes from employees' paychecks, sending them to the proper government agencies, and other employer tax obligations. The major employer-paid taxes (FICA, federal unemployment, and state unemployment taxes) will be explained later in this section.*
>
> *The Federal Insurance Contributions Act (FICA) provides for a federal system of old-age, survivors, disability, and hospital*

insurance. The first three are financed by the social security tax, while hospital insurance is financed by the Medicare tax.

To learn more about the five major benefits covered by Social Security taxes (retirement, disability, family benefits, survivors and Medicare), please refer to the Social Security Administration's Web site.

Employers must withhold social security and Medicare taxes from employees' wages and pay a matching amount. These taxes have different rates and only the social security tax has a wage base limit. There is no wage base limit for Medicare tax; all covered wages are subject to Medicare tax.

The Federal Unemployment Tax Act (FUTA), together with state unemployment systems, provides for payments of unemployment compensation to workers who have lost their jobs. Most employers pay both a federal and a state unemployment tax. Only the employer pays FUTA tax; it is not deducted from the employee's wages. Employers can take a credit against FUTA tax for amounts paid into state unemployment funds. This credit cannot be more than 5.4 percent of taxable wages. Those entitled to the maximum 5.4 percent credit have an effective FUTA tax rate of 0.8 percent after the credit. The IRS has tests to determine whether a particular business must pay FUTA tax.

State unemployment taxes are also paid by the employer and are not deducted from the employee's wages. Each state has a different rate and different wage limits from which the taxes are calculated.

When you hire employees, you must carry worker's compensation insurance for them. This covers employees who are injured on the job; the purpose of this insurance is to avoid lawsuits stemming from employees who are hurt while performing their job duties. Worker's compensation insurance is administered by both federal and state statutes.

Examples of an Employee Hiring Agreement and an Independent Contractor Agreement can be found on the companion CD-ROM.

Managing Employees

When you started your business, you had to learn new skills and abilities to become a business owner. When you hire employees, you will need to learn additional skills as the boss. You must train your employees to handle your business according to your policies and procedures and ensure that their actions reflect favorably on your company. Each of your employees is now a representative of your company.

On your new employee's first day on the job, you will need to spend some time going over your operating procedures and policies. An employee handbook or written instructions will help. The new sitter may accompany you on your rounds that day to observe your methods, and you can see them in action. If you have any new client interviews scheduled, this is an excellent time to work with your new employee on your method of data collection, and it will you an opportunity to see the new hire's skills with clients.

You might consider hiring a back-up sitter or working out an agreement with another sitting company to provide reciprocal services if one of you becomes incapacitated or is on vacation. In that case, it is not unreasonable for each of you to work a pet sitting appointment together so that you are familiar and comfortable with the other sitter's style. If you do not agree with the other sitter's methods, do not partner with them — they could harm your reputation with your clients!

Your clients and employees should understand that the pet sitting contract is between your company and your client, not an individual sitter. Clients may have sitter preferences, and it is reasonable to honor those requests. However, it is never acceptable for the sitter to contact the client to work independently with them; it is not acceptable for the client to contact the sitter to make private arrangements for service. You may avoid this complication by having your sitters sign a non-compete agreement as part of their conditions of hire. If the sitter has other services or products that they offer, they should not try to sell them to the client while in an official capacity as the client's pet sitter. They should be focused on the job they are doing for your company.

As the boss you can be warm and friendly, but you must always remain in charge. There is a natural barrier between employee and boss, and you should be careful not to try to become too involved in your employees' lives or blur the line between friendship and authority. Your workers must respect you. Everything that happens in the business is ultimately your responsibility. While you want to be open to feedback and ideas, be careful not to become the therapist or allow yourself to be taken advantage of. If you are too involved with your employees' problems, you may be too accommodating about lateness, handling personal business, or child care problems. Always send the message that you expect employees to behave professionally while on the job.

As a manager you must also remain aware of the health and problems of your employees. A pattern of sickness or absenteeism may signal a deeper problem that you might need to address before it gets out of hand. If you ignore psychological or substance-abuse problems, they could directly impact morale and productivity.

Employee policies or an employee handbook can help you and your new hires understand what is expected of them and how you will handle problems. You should address such issues as how you will handle excessive tardiness or requests for days off, the fact that any alcohol or substance abuse is forbidden (and grounds for immediate dismissal), and how you will handle interpersonal conflicts.

Because pet sitters in a business tend to have little contact with each other, you may not experience many personnel clashes or negativity that leads to poor morale. However, these issues are possible and should be nipped in the bud; many people suffer for a long time in a toxic environment because the boss is too busy or oblivious or helpless to make a change. You do not want to be that boss. If you employ multiple workers, listen for conflicts. Help your employees feel secure that you will listen to their issues, and do your best to address problems. When two employees are locked in a conflict, make sure you listen without bias to both sides before taking action.

Success through Motivation

You are in charge of motivating your employees. Motivation will carry employees through boredom, burnout, and day-to-day stress. You can motivate someone through positive or negative reinforcement. The negative reinforcement will only work for a short time. If you offer an employee harsh discipline and criticism, they might respond short-term but will revert to negative behaviors or eventually quit. Avoidance of punishment is not the behavior you want to encourage.

People are genuinely engaged and enthusiastic about working for a company that values them as an individual and for what they can contribute. Though being fairly paid is a motivator in itself, people also need positive reinforcement. Your encouragement can be as simple as noting things your employee does well or specific situations where they have gone above and beyond what is expected. Thank them in person, give them a card, or write them a note or e-mail. Praise and recognition will boost their morale more than any other non-financial motivator.

There are other ways to engage your employees and keep them satisfied with their jobs. Tokens of recognition such as gift certificates, movie tickets, company T-shirts and bags, or gift baskets can show them how much you appreciate them. Keeping open communication lines can help them to share ideas and feel more closely attached to the business. When possible, let the employees make their own decisions and suggest changes to improve the business. You may find their insight valuable This is an excellent tactic when employees seem bored with their current responsibilities. Consider expanding their roles to take on more challenging tasks; you may free yourself up to do more of the tasks you like to do. Since employees feel more connected to a business in which they feel they have some authority, be sure you do not micromanage them. You may need to monitor a new hire closely, but after he or she has proven themselves trustworthy, let the person have some latitude in managing his or her own work.

Pet sitters may not have much interaction with other sitters; you may want to plan business meetings. This can be as informal as a pizza party, or a coffee-and–doughnuts morning meeting. Give your employees the chance to interact with each other. In a staff meeting you can address any complaints or concerns, describe new procedures, explain new policies, and introduce new employees. You can recognize employees who have done well and encourage all workers to be enthusiastic about their work.

If you are consistent in managing employees, you treat each person fairly while appreciating their differences. By offering the support each person needs to succeed, you will be able to retain good employees.

"Our perfect companions never have fewer than four feet."

~Colette

Operating Procedures

The procedures in this chapter are designed to get your business up and running quickly and get you out into the neighborhood caring for pets. These procedures are designed by dozens of pet sitting professionals who have discovered successful processes through trial and error. When you have a specific process for each task, you are more efficient and less likely to miss an important step. If you hire others, you can train them from the start on how you would like them to perform your business, and you are ensured they will all follow the same procedures. These are only a starting point for you to find what works for you. As you become more familiar with these everyday activities, you will likely refine these ideas to fit your business.

Business Policies

As a business owner, you will need to make general policies and procedures to ensure your business runs well. For example, when a client wants you to take care of the dog but that you can ignore the cat since cats are self-sufficient, you can tell the client that your company policy does not allow you to neglect any animal (and that you must be paid for your work).

General policies you will want to consider include:

- **Appointment hours.** Will you set specific parameters or will you be available whenever requested?

- **Office hours.** When can clients reach you, and how soon can they expect a reply to a message or e-mail?

- **Handling payments.** When is payment required? Will clients have to pay a deposit beforehand and the balance when the work is completed? Will you have a grace period? How will you handle late accounts or returned checks?

- **Pet Immunizations.** Will you require proof of immunizations and veterinarian care before taking on a pet sitting engagement so that you avoid spreading disease from one animal to another?

- **Non-sitting appointments.** Do you plan to charge for appointments when you are not providing animal care, such as an initial client interview or when you pick up keys? Will you offer discounts if the client leaves a key with you?

- **Alternative sitters:** Will you share sitting responsibility with other sitters or provide a backup for an emergency? How will you handle multiple sitters taking care of the same pet or family members who share pet sitting duties?

- **Pet identification:** Will you require all pets to wear an identification collar? What other identification methods will you expect?

- **Last-minute reservations:** Will you agree to take care of an animal at the last minute — even if it means that you will not be able to meet with the owner beforehand? Will you charge extra for these requests?

- **Holiday sitting:** Do you plan to charge more for appointments on holidays, or will you treat those as regular visits?

As your business builds, you will likely find more issues for which you will need a policy. There is more than one way to run a sitting business, and you will find what works for you and what you will need to manage closely.

Case Study: Christi Marks

Christi Marks

All Tails Pet Care

Green Bay, Wisconsin

Time management is problem area to avoid. You must be sure you can commit to the times and sits for each client. You never want to book so many appointments that you cannot get to all the pets in time, leaving animals waiting. We want them comfortable in their homes, not miserable because they cannot get outside.

Being insured is a must. If anything happens to these pets or the home, then you are covered. So many things can arise. For example, a leash can break while on a walk, and the dog could run away and get hurt. You could lose the client's house key and have to have a locksmith come to get in the house so you can sit for the pets. Come rain or shine, if clients need you for sitting, you have to find a way to get to the house. I have walked dogs in cold weather, in pouring rain, and in blowing snow.

I schedule a "meet and greet" before I take on any pet sitting jobs. This allows me to meet the clients and the pets and get a feel for what they need. This is also the time the customer fills out the paperwork — everything from medical information to the house information to the pet sitting contract. I want to know where the water shutoff is, the breaker box, the cleaning supplies and all other information. They sign veterinary releases so that I have all their vet information on hand. I then enter all the information into QuickBooks. I have a file cabinet with a separate file folder for each client containing all the information I might need.

Basic Office Procedure

When you receive a request for service, a group of activities that will vary little throughout your business is set in motion. Here is a look at the basic office procedure — specifics of the procedure are found in the sections below.

1. You receive a call from a client. You fill out a customer information card/form.

2. If this is a new client, you schedule a client appointment as described in Chapter 7.

3. Note the assignment on your calendar.

4. If you have employees, contact the appropriate sitter and assign the job.

5. Note the sitter assignment on the monthly schedule.

6. Add the monthly schedule and client information to a pending jobs stack or bin.

7. Check the pending jobs stack on a daily basis to discover any completed assignments.

8. File finished job information, or note it in the file if you are using a computer to manage this information.

9. Check the job-finished column on the appropriate sitter's schedule.

10. Send invoice to client and note it in your accounts receivable file.

11. When payment is received, note the information in your accounting file and sitter schedule sheet.

12. On a weekly or monthly basis, pay sitters for completed assignments. Note the date and amount they were paid in their sitter file.

How to Manage a Client's Records & Keys

Security is an issue of increasing concern in today's society. When you are contracted to take care of an animal, you are responsible not only for the pet, but also for the home. You must keep the client's information secure and the keys safe from theft or misuse.

Client records must be stored in cabinets that can be locked. Many pet sitters work from their own homes, so the sitter should keep the pet owner's information separate from household records. Client information should always be protected. When you are talking with friends, you should be careful not to mention the details of your sitting arrangements, information about your clients or their pets, or details about their homes and lives. Never mention when a client is absent from his or her home.

The best way to keep client records secure is to assign them an identification number in your accounting program. Put that identifier number on their primary house key, along with a pet's name. If you have received duplicate keys, make sure the backup key has only their identification number and is stored and locked in a separate location. Store the keys and files in a file cabinet that locks, and make sure your computer programs are password-protected. If you post on internet job or message boards about a specific situation, never use the client's name or pet's name — only "the dog" or "the cat."

When a client no longer needs your services, the pet records should be destroyed. Do not just throw the information into the trash; use a shredder to destroy the information. Even if the client asks you to throw away the spare key, always return it to them and get a receipt stating you have returned the key.

How to Manage A Daily & Monthly Schedule

Maintaining the daily and monthly schedule is the most critical of your activities. If you miss something, a pet's health and safety are at stake. If you overbook, your week will become stressful. If you have under-booked, your slow periods will cause you anxiety.

When you agree with a client to provide service on a specific date, you should record the booking dates on a calendar, appointment book, or PDA. This allows you to quickly see the dates and times open for appointments. However, this does not provide sufficient information to organize each day's visits. For this reason, it is important to note more information on a monthly schedule form.

Case Study: Miranda Murdock

Miranda Murdock

My Pet's Buddy

Greenwood, Louisiana

To keep track of client and animal information, I use Microsoft® Office Accounting 2007, but for a long time I used Microsoft® Accounting Express, a free program that has nearly everything a small business needs.

The only reason I upgraded was to get the "memorized documents" feature, which is not a necessity. I found that by educating myself on different programs I have been able to modify the accounting program to store all required info, and using that in conjunction with the computer calendar and business contact manager, I have everything covered. I keep my paper files because I want to have original signatures on file.

I use Microsoft ® Outlook on my desktop and synchronize it with my PDA, which also has a satellite navigation program and receiver. Tentative bookings are labeled in one color, solid bookings not yet invoiced are in a different color, and after I send the invoice, I change it to another color.

The monthly schedule is the place to record details of each booking so that you are prepared for daily visits. This schedule can be kept on a pad of paper or in a computer file, whichever you find most convenient. For each client you have booked during that month, you will record the following information:

- Total number of visits
- The date of the first and last visits (mark the last visit so that it stands out)
- Any special instructions or comments from the client
- The total fee
- Whether or not you have a signed service contract from the client
- Whether you have the client's key
- Whether or not the client has paid the fee or deposit (if required)

Plan your daily schedule the night before so that you are organized and ready to go in the morning. Think through the day and organize your service visits, business chores, and client appointments for maximum efficiency and to be sure you have not missed anything. For example, imagine you have scheduled a client visit at noon. When you look at your monthly appointment sheet, though, you realize that this is the day of the week when you water the Smiths' entire lawn. You will need to plan extra time to meet both commitments.

Writing down the daily schedule can be as simple as a longhand list on a tablet of paper. You can also use a daily planner, an appointment book, or a PDA device to schedule your day. Start by pulling all the details of your bookings from your service agreements and your pending monthly schedule. Review the commitments for the next day and check them against a map to determine the most efficient, gas-saving route. If any of your agreements have special stipulations, such as being at the house at a certain time of day, be sure to plan that into your schedule. Then note a list of the tasks you will need to do the next day, in the order or time period you will need to do them.

Because you are ultimately responsible for the well-being of a number of animals, double check your agreements to be sure all visits have been properly accounted for. Review your monthly schedule and place a check next to the corresponding entry in the daily schedule. Then review the monthly schedule again and see if any of the entries indicate that this is the last day of service for any of the clients. The last day of your visits is a good time to do something extra for the client to cement your reputation for quality service. In addition, you may want to leave the client a payment envelope for their convenience.

How to Handle Calls for Service

The first time a client calls to request your service, you have an excellent opportunity to make a positive impression. Whenever possible, answer the phone and put some warmth in your voice by smiling during the conversation. The client will want to know about your rates, services, and policies, but they also want to know that you are someone who can be trusted to love and nurture their pets while they are gone.

Pet sitting remains a new concept for many people, so prepare a short speech about your work and your offerings. This short speech will also be handy when someone asks you at a party, "What do you do?" and then looks at you blankly when you say, "I am a pet sitter." Here is a sample response for a caller. If you keep this response close to your phone, you will be prepared.

Caller: "I just saw your Web site online while I was looking for someone to watch my pets, and I am wondering if you can tell me a little about your business."

Sitter: "My business provides personalized care for dogs (or other animal) in their owners' homes. We believe it is better for animals to remain in a familiar environment while you are away from home. Our sitters follow your pet care routine as closely as possible. This includes feeding and watering, exercising, and any special care, like giving your pet medication. We also spend time just playing with your pet or petting them, so they get the attention they need while their owners are gone. We keep an eye on your house to be sure all is well while you are gone, too. We will bring in your mail and newspapers, water your plants, alternate lights so it appears that you are home, and close or open curtains and blinds. The sitters are insured and bonded, so you can feel secure in their work. Our fees are based on the number and type of pets and the number of visits and extra services you request. We ask that you give us three days' notice for pet visits, and we start with an initial meeting with you so that I can meet your pets and we can complete a service agreement. If you can tell me the types of services you need and a little about your pets, I can give you an estimate right now."

How to Handle Customer Complaints

Even the best pet sitters might have to deal with customer complaints at times. Because pet sitting is a service-oriented business, you must focus on customer satisfaction. This does not mean that you have to give in to unreasonable demands, but it does mean that you have to respond to problems with tact, fairness, and honesty. Always respond to complaints quickly, and keep the client involved in the progress toward resolution.

Case Study: Terri Randall

Terri Randall

Creature Comforts Pet Care

Sheridan, Wyoming

Regardless of whether I think the client has a valid point or not, my philosophy for handling customer complaints is always the same. Listen, sympathize, be understanding, and try to resolve the situation to our mutual benefit.

This does not always mean apologizing. If it was my fault or if I was some how derelict in my duties, then I apologize and make no excuses for myself. We are all human, and I think the way you approach the individual situation makes a difference.

If a client is dissatisfied, do not become discouraged. Hear their view with an open mind, and make sure you understand the scope of the problem. If the problem concerns a pet sitter who works for you, let the client know you will contact the employee promptly and get to the bottom of the matter. Then express your regret that the client is unhappy. This does not mean you are apologizing for something you did not do or admitting wrongdoing; it means you are in business to make your customer happy and you regret that they are unhappy.

Determine whether the client has a legitimate complaint and find out the cause of the problem. Was it miscommunication that led to you feeding the dog the wrong food? Was it an accident that you left the door open to an off-limits room, and now cat hair is everywhere? Finding the cause of the problem may not help the situation, especially when you have to say, "I am sorry that your dog did not get his pills, but you never mentioned the medication when I interviewed you." You can use that problem as a way to improve your business in the future. For example, add a checklist item to your interview agenda to ask each potential client about medical needs.

After you have sorted out the issue, you must determine how to resolve things. If the complaint is justified, you might reduce or waive fees for the service or you might offer a free service in the future. If you are liable for damages, contact your insurance company and file a claim. However, if the complaint is not justified, tactfully and clearly state your position and your reasons for your conclusion. Even if a customer becomes upset, make sure you maintain your professionalism and strive for a resolution that will be beneficial.

Case Study: Miranda Murdock

Miranda Murdock

My Pet's Buddy

Greenwood, LA

I have had few complaints, but I listen (or read, since most of my correspondence with clients is via e-mail) and determine what caused the complaint.

Did I misunderstand what the client wanted? Did I make a mistake? In those cases, I apologize, offer a credit toward their next booking, and then figure out how to prevent that kind of miscommunication in the future. I would only offer a refund in the most extreme cases, and only if I were negligent. If the client just seems to be unsatisfied, with no specific complaint, then I try to set them up with someone they will be happier with. I think it is better to focus on avoiding complaints, rather having to deal with them happening. The best way I have found to do this is to always leave specific, honest notes about anything that transpires during a visit or a walk. I include all the details of what happened, what I did about it, and why I did it.

At some point, you may run into an unreasonable client. If the owner makes too many demands, finds fault with a good job, or gives you a sense of danger or unease, you are justified in terminating the work relationship. In this case, as well as any situation that has the potential to escalate, you are wise to follow up your termination discussion with an e-mail or letter than puts down in writing the reasons for ending the sitting agreement.

How to Handle Delinquent Accounts

You may occasionally face the frustration of having to handle non-payment or delinquent accounts. Since payment for pet sitting may be due when the service is rendered, you might provide a bill or leave one at the home when the assignment is finished. If you are accepting a long assignment, or working with a new client, you may want to ask for a deposit on the fees.

To protect yourself in advance, make sure your contract or agreement with the client contains a clause stating that payment is due in 30 days of service. You should also include a statement on your policy for returned checks. For example, you would expect the client to pay any fees associated with their returned check. Many businesses also assess a charge of $10-$20 for each returned check. Putting these policies into the contract will help you if you need to take a case to court to force a client to pay.

Most clients will not jeopardize a good pet sitting relationship by not paying a bill. Try calling the client first to ask them to stop by and pay the bill or to drop it in the mail. If the issue was a returned check, you may know that the check has been returned before they do, and it is likely there was a simple oversight on the client's part that they will quickly resolve. If you do not receive payment after two calls, it is time to put something in writing. This is an appropriate time to use your business stationery. State the dates of service and services performed and politely but firmly request payment within five days. Writing a letter like this requires you to have kept good records on the services provided and the invoices you have sent. A sample letter is shown below and is also included on the companion CD-ROM.

Delinquent Account Notice

Dear (Client Name):

On reviewing our records, I have found that there is a delinquent balance on your account in the amount of $________. This balance is for pet sitting services provided by Jane Doe of Acme Pet Sitting, Inc. from January 1 through January 15, 20__, which was billed to you on January 15. While this may be an oversight on your part, we appreciate your prompt attention to this matter. We enjoy caring for your pets and would like to continue providing our services to you. Please remit payment to us within five (5) days.

Best Regards,

Acme Pet Sitting, Inc.

If letters and phone calls do not resolve the problem, a last resort might be taking the client to small claims court. A small claims case is one in which a low amount of money is involved. Though the threshold varies from state to state, somewhere around $1,500. In small claims court, a judge will listen to both sides of the case and determine who is at fault. These cases are inexpensive and the process is not difficult, but you will need to reserve time to be at court for the hearing.

If the judge awards you the small claims case, the client receives a lien on their property such as a house or a business. The court decision may also require the party at fault to pay court costs for hearing the case. The amount due must be paid in full for the lien to be removed from the person's record. If the person tries to sell the property while the lien is filed, the lien must be paid before the sale is final.

It can be uncomfortable to pursue a client for non-payment of your pet sitting services, but it is money you have earned and deserve to receive. If you have provided legitimate services and have not received what is owed to you, you have the right to be heard in court and to collect on the debt.

How to Handle Emergencies

The tragedies of the September 11 terrorist attacks and of Hurricane Katrina have made many people more aware of the need for disaster preparedness plans for their families and their pets. No matter where you live, your area is susceptible to some type of natural disaster. The United States suffers more than 150,000 household fires, 10,000 violent thunderstorms, 5,000 floods, 800 tornadoes, and numerous forest fires, hurricanes, floods, and earthquakes each year.

A pet sitter is responsible for the health and well-being of the pets in his or her care, even in a disaster or emergency. For that reason, you must prepare several plans: a plan for taking care of the pets if you physically cannot get to them, a plan for evacuating the animals if an evacuation order has been given, and a plan for placing the animals if the home becomes unlivable because of an emergency. As a professional, you should also have a backup plan in case you are incapacitated and cannot care for the animals. When you first meet with a client, communicate these plans to him or her. Knowing that you are prepared for emergencies will add to their confidence in you.

If you live in a part of the country where bad weather such as snow and ice storms occur, it is wise to ask the client to leave a key with a nearby neighbor who can stop by the house to check on the pets if it is impossible for you to drive there. You can reassure the client that you would request the neighbor's help only in an extreme emergency. If you become sick or injured and cannot make your pet sitting rounds, you should have a backup sitter identified in advance who can take over for you. You may never need to use their services, but if you do, their help is essential.

If you arrive for a pet sitting appointment and see signs of a break-in, do not enter the house. Always trust your gut feeling if you see signs of danger. Call the police from a neighbor's home or your cell phone. Wait for the police to arrive and then check to be sure the animals are safe. If you must go on to your next appointments, check with the police officers to be sure it is safe to enter the home later in the day.

Case Study: Terri Randall

Stephanie Erway

Furr Pet Sake, Inc.

Denver, Colorado

Safety is important on the job. I used to carry a stun gun. Now I just keep my cell phone on me at all times. I also use a hands-free Bluetooth. If I need to contact the police because of something happening, I can just press one button and the police are automatically called.

I also have another sitter that works for me, and if I am going into an area that I do not feel safe in, she knows where I am. If she does not hear from me in a reasonable time she will call the police. If I am scared, I do not do the job. Know the areas that you sit in and be choosy about what areas you are willing to go in. This is your business, and you can make up any rules you like.

When you are on a pet sitting appointment, you should check the home to be sure there are no problems that will precipitate an emergency, such as finding a burst pipe or a non-functioning air conditioner. Your contract with the client should authorize you to handle emergencies such as these; if the contract is not explicit, you will need to call the owner and ask for instructions. When the sitting visit is in an apartment or condominium, your first step is to call the association or office for repairs. If you are sitting at a house, you should call the repair service if you have authorization to do so. It is possible that a fire, furnace problem, or some other emergency will make the home unsafe for the pets. In this case, you should consult with the owners and relieve their anxiety by offering suggestions, such as a kennel that you recommend, a veterinarian that will care for the pets for a few days, or offering your own home if that is possible for you.

Ask your clients to put together an evacuation kit for their animals and leave it near a door. The kit should contain all the provisions the animals will need if taken to another location, including proof of ownership, a recent picture of the animal, and veterinary and immunization records.

The kit for small domestic pets might contain:

1. Crate, carrier, cage, or portable aquarium for each pet large enough for the pet to turn around in and cat carriers large enough for a small litter box
2. Pet Identification Forms for each pet with photos attached
3. Collar and leash for all pets (including cats) with identification and rabies tags on all collars (For birds and reptiles this may be a leg tag; for amphibians and fish, this may be a sticker on the aquarium.)
4. Vaccination records of each pet
5. Three-week supply of each pet's medications
6. Sedatives for pets that frighten easily
7. Disposable litter boxes and scoop
8. Extra cat litter
9. Plastic bags, paper towels, and cleaning supplies
10. Three-week supply of food for each pet
11. Manual can opener
12. Food and water bowls for each pet
13. Supply of drinking water
14. Toys or blankets the pet will find familiar

15. Towels
16. Grooming items
17. Detailed instructions for animal care and rescue workers
18. Copy of emergency numbers and family evacuation plan
19. Copy of veterinarian's information
20. Flashlight and batteries
21. Pet first aid kit: include bandaging material, antiseptic ointment, alcohol, gloves, tweezers, muzzle, and gauze
22. List of all area hotels accepting pets
23. First-aid books for pets and humans

Reptiles may also need:

1. Water bowl for soaking
2. Spray bottle for misting
3. Extra bags or newspapers
4. Heating pad
5. Battery-operated heating source or other appropriate heat source
6. Extra batteries
7. Appropriate handling gloves/supplies

The kit for livestock and barnyard animals might contain:

1. Seven- to ten-day supply of feed and water
2. Batteries for flashlight and radio
3. Copies of veterinary records and proof of ownership
4. Cotton halter
5. Duct tape
6. Emergency contact list
7. Flashlight
8. Heavy gloves (leather)
9. Instructions
10. Diet: record the diet for the animals.
11. Medications: record the dose and frequency for each medication. Provide veterinary and pharmacy contact information for refills.
12. Knife (sharp, all-purpose)
13. Fly spray
14. Grooming brushes
15. Heavy leather gloves
16. Hoof knife

17. Hoof nippers
18. Hoof pick
19. Hoof rasp
20. Leg wraps and horse blankets
21. Maps of local area and alternate evacuation routes in case of road closures
22. Nose leads
23. Plastic trash cans with lids (to store water)
24. Portable livestock panels
25. Radio (solar and battery operated)
26. Rope or lariat
27. Shovel
28. Water buckets
29. Whip, prods
30. Wire cutters

Being prepared for anything will make you more valuable as a sitter and more composed when emergencies arise. Make sure any sitters who work for you are competent to follow all your procedures and to handle problems and emergencies.

"The problem with loving is that pets don't last long enough and people last too long."

Promoting the Business

Finding Customers

Where do you find the people who need someone to look after their pets? There are two ways to find clients: through word of mouth and through marketing at places pet lovers will likely see your business name.

The best way to find new clients is by producing loyal, satisfied customers who will tell others about your services. When you start your business, you may perform a few discount jobs for friends just for the recognition and experience. When those friends speak highly of your service, people will begin to associate you with loving, careful pet care. Word-of-mouth advertising may take a little longer, but people are more likely to use a service provider who is recommended by a friend than someone they have picked out of a phone book. Give your current clients a supply of your business cards or flyers and ask those clients to share them with others. Pet lovers tend to know other pet lovers, and sooner or later the question, "Who takes care of Fido when you are gone?" will come up. You might even offer your clients a discount or gift certificate for each new customer they recommended you to. If someone has given you a good recommendation, always send them a thank-you card.

Your own self-promotion and the recommendations of friends will get your name out in the public eye. If you work another job, let your coworkers know you have a part-time sitting business. Instruct your family and friends in the best way to describe your business when they bring up your profession to others. Strike up conversations with people in pet stores, pet groomers, while waiting for the vet, or at the dog park.

Pet sitting is a business where your customers will come to you because you are local, loving, professional, and recommended. In contrast to other businesses, people do not want a big, impersonal company sending out an anonymous service provider. They want to know the sitter and have a good feeling about the sitter's personal style. This is a benefit to you as you build your business. Your skills, love for animals, and personality are more important than a huge multi-level company.

Case Study: Miranda Murdock

Miranda Murdock

My Pet's Buddy

Greenwood, Louisiana

My customers find me, and many of them have come from the Internet. I think a Web site is the most important advertising tool, and insuring that you come up high in searches is critical.

In addition, I do postings on the popular online community boards, such as Craigslist and pet sitting directories. Next would be veterinarian referrals, or even if the doctor does not make a specific referral, the client sees my information in the lobby. Other clients have come by word of mouth, and I have business cards and car advertising.

One method that has provided visibility is my car signs, although I modified them so that there is also a business card dispenser on each one. People can take my cards even when I am not there to give them out. There is some controversy about having car signs: Does it tell would be burglars that the house is empty? Or does it tell them someone is stopping by the house regularly, and there might be a huge, mean dog inside? However, I have had only had one client object to the signs.

Case Study: Miranda Murdock

This might be something you want to get a law enforcement perspective on, since it is controversial. A note about veterinarian referrals — some people say they have met resistance from the veterinary technicians and office workers at the office because they also do pet sitting. The way I have found to ease that reluctance is to talk about my availability for daily dog walks, when the technicians are at work and unavailable. I have had cards made specifically advertising dog-walking services, with no mention of pet sitting, specifically for that situation.

Marketing and Advertising

Marketing has an intimidating "big business" feel to it, but marketing is the process of letting people know you are open for business and telling them why they should hire you. There are unlimited ways to tell people about your business. Your message must stand out to be heard because potential customers are bombarded with numerous messages every day.

In the first few chapters, you analyzed the attributes of good pet sitters and thought through what you can offer to potential clients. When you build your marketing and advertising plan, you will use that information to tell your clients why they should hire you rather than someone else.

First decide what your public image will look like. How do you want people to see your business? This is the "look and feel" of your company logo, business cards, letterhead, flyers or brochures, Web site, and any other media advertising. Make sure your image reflects you well; if you do not take care of snakes, do not put them in your logo. If you want to look homey, folksy, and comfortable, your logo should reflect that. Few of us are graphic designers, but having a public image that looks the same no matter how it is used will help people remember your business. If your flyers have one look and your business cards have a completely different look, it will be hard for customers to connect the two. Imagine the best-case scenario: a dog owner finds your business card with the cute animal logo and the eye-catching green text at the veterinarian's office. A few days later, she sees a flyer at the grocery store that shows the same logo and text. Next, she opens her newspaper and sees your ad with that cute logo again. "Hmmm," she thinks, "This must be a great company. I am seeing them all over the place."

There are many computer applications, such as Microsoft® Publisher or PowerPoint, Adobe® Photoshop, and others that allow you to create a logo of your own. If you have an inclination to computer work, designing your own images and stationery can be fun. If not, the Internet is full of discount business supply printers who can help you easily create your own look, print your business cards, forms, and stationery, and mail everything to your house. It is cheap, easy, and has a professional appeal. If you are not one for computers or the Internet, your hometown likely has a business printing company that can take care of all your needs. In any case, shop around; prices can vary widely.

Each of the following marketing opportunities will help you grow your business:

1. A selection of printed materials and places to distribute them. A flyer or brochure that explains your services, basic policies, credentials and experience will create interest with your clients. Include a photo of yourself for a personal touch. You can distribute these flyers anywhere, but pay particular attention to pet and feed stores, veterinarians' offices and animal hospitals, dog or cat shows, pet associations, animal shelters, and trade shows. Other places to distribute your flyers and business cards include:

- School or office bulletin boards
- Humane societies

- "Welcome Wagon" programs for new residents
- Local businesses
- Clubs and non-profit organizations
- Travel agencies
- Apartment and condominium complexes

2. Paid advertising. Try taking out an ad in your local phone book. Make sure you have an eye-catching design in the yellow pages. An advertisement in local newspapers can be reasonable, but you will need to renew the ad regularly. If local pet associations or pet professionals have a periodic newsletter, contact the publication to ask for an ad or write an article for their newsletter. You can also place classified ads in specialty magazines, specifically those dealing with animal topics.

3. Web site. It is common knowledge that more people find information, businesses, and professionals through Web site searches than any other method. By maintaining a Web site for your business, you will offer your clients and potential customers valuable information without ever having to pick up the phone. A client can see all the details about your business, including policies and hours, and this will encourage them to give you a call. At a minimum, your Web site should include the following:

- Your name, phone number and e-mail address
- Your company's history and your experience
- Information about the services you offer and the prices

- A list of animals you are able to care for

- Links to any organizations, associations, or professional references

- Why someone should hire a pet sitter and why that sitter should be you

Web sites can offer even more, though. You can provide testimonials from satisfied clients, and offer contact information so that a potential client can check references — just make sure you have permission to do so. You might publish articles or a newsletter on pet care or sitting topics to establish yourself as a knowledgeable leader in pet sitting. Some pet sitting sites offer a calendar of available sitting dates, an online pet information form, a reservation request, and a comment form.

If you do not have the skills or inclination to build your own Web site from free and easy to use Internet tools, there are many Web designers who can help. A simple Web site can cost as little as a few hundred dollars, and this is money well-spent on your marketing efforts.

4. Press Releases. Press releases are free publicity. When you open your business, ask the newspapers and online sources to announce it to the world. Anytime you or an employee win an award, receive an accreditation, open a new line of business, or achieve something brilliant, you want the world to know. The uniqueness of your news may trigger interest from the newspaper or another writer to run a feature article on your business.

News releases help you stay in the public eye. If newsworthy and positive things continually occur in your business, people will remember your name and see you as an expert or a valuable resource. The type of news you release will also help your public image. If you, as a business leader, are involved in charity work, announce what you are doing. This shows your humanitarian values and brings attention to your favorite charities. If you partner with other businesses for a larger purpose, such as building a think tank of business leaders, you will emphasize your role as a leader and an essential member of the community.

Anyone can write and submit a press or news release; the media will choose the ones they want to publish. However, the release should offer readers an interesting news angle and should not be written as an advertising piece. Instead, the release should tell the news story.

Your press release needs a catchy title. Many editors do not read past the title line of a press release; if the title has not caught his or her interest, the rest of the release will not be read. The title should be short and concise and contain the name of the organization.

Press releases are written in the "inverted pyramid" style, with the most important information in the first paragraph, and the least important information in the final sentences. It must answer all the basic journalistic questions: who, what, when, where, and how. The entire release should be no more than two pages, and the writing should capture the reader's attention from the first line. In the last paragraph, write a brief overview of your organization, labeling it "Note to Editors" or "About Us."

The press release writer should be sure that all typos and spelling mistakes are corrected before sending to an editor. It is also important to review the contact information, such as addresses and phone numbers, to be sure those are completely accurate. If a reader wants to contact you, it should be easy to do so.

Here is an example of how a press release will read (see the companion CD-ROM for a blank version):

Sample Press Release

For Immediate Release:

Title: Loving Pet Care for Holiday Travelers

June 1, 2008 (Press Release) — For Immediate Release

Chicago/June 1, 2008 — A professional dog walking and pet sitting service, Purry Care Pet Sitting, now has service covering the Chicago area just in time for the holidays. Jane Doe provides expert care as a licensed pet sitting professional.

Purry Care provides a variety of services for dogs, cats, and other small animals, including private and group dog walks and doggie play groups, cat visits, in-home overnight sitting, private boarding, day care, home care and pet taxi service.

The demand for professional pet sitting and dog walking services is at an all-time high. Pet ownership is rising, pet owners are working longer hours and traveling more for business and personal reasons than ever before, and pet owners are moving away from kenneling their pets because of health concerns, making alternatives like Purry Care more attractive.

As part of the grand opening celebration through July 31, Purry Care is offering a 10 percent discount off each new client's first service. More information, a complete list of service areas and contact information are available at Purry Care's Web site at **www.purrycare.com** or by calling 555-555-5115.

CONTACT:

Jane Doe
Purry Care Pet Sitting
PO Box 1000
Chicago, IL 60610
PHONE 555-555-5115

###

5.Television and Radio. These advertising media can be expensive and intimidating, but they can also be rewarding. A radio commercial that plays during rush hour will be played at just the time when most people are listening to the radio; it also targets people who are away from home for part of each day. Television commercials offer an image of respectability and prosperity. If you decide to explore these advertising routes, be sure the broadcast area and station fit the demographics you want to work for, or your advertising efforts are in vain. An interesting news angle can develop from a well-planned advertising campaign. Your ad might spark the interest of journalists who could develop a news story, or even want to interview you. Keep your mind open to the possibilities.

Case Study: Terri Randall 

Terri Randall

Creature Comforts Pet Care

Sheridan, Wyoming

I live in a rural area with a smaller population than other pet sitters' areas. My entire county (comprised of several towns) is about 20,000 people. Here, everyone knows everyone, and word travels fast.

The advertising and marketing strategies that have been most successful for me were the personal contacts I have made with others in the pet industry. They know and trust me, so they refer people to me, and vice versa. In a larger, more metropolitan area, that might not work as well. That, together with my Web site, has been the most beneficial to me.

I did all kinds of advertising when I started: print, radio, and "face time" with other pet-related businesses. I would visit vet offices, groomers, pet supply stores, and trainers to introduce myself and leave business cards and brochures. I volunteered at our local shelter and made good contacts there as well.

Here are a few other ideas for getting attention for your business:

- Design posters and place them on community bulletin boards.
- Place ads in programs, bulletins, and booklets that offer advertising space. Sports teams, schools, and social clubs often provide a place for your advertising.
- Print your logo on T-shirts, sweatshirts, or doggie wraps, and pass them out to your clients. Wear your own shirt often in public.
- Produce pens, key chains, or other promotional items and distribute them.

- Provide gift certificates for fund-raising events.
- Advertise at hospital bulletin boards or at the offices of foot, ankle, or orthopedic doctors. People with broken feet cannot walk dogs.
- Leave a business card with each of the people you do business with each day: your beauty salon, gas station, dry cleaner, dentist, and doctor.
- When you return a book to the library, stick a business card in the pages. Someone who checks out the book next may be looking for a reliable sitter.
- Put a magnetic sign on your car, or spring for personalized license plates. People will see your advertisement all day long.
- Check into direct mail coupons programs run by agencies such as Super Shopper and Val-Pak®.
- Explore the possibility of placing ads on the back of local grocery store receipts.
- Post your business information on Internet business listings such as Craigslist.
- List your business on online pet sitting directories such as Pet Sitters International.

Associations and Organizations

If you pursue membership in organizations and associations related to animal care and pet sitting, you increase your personal resources. Pet sitting organizations can put you in touch with thousands of professionals in your line of business. These contacts can offer advice, support, tips, accreditations programs, insurance, and new jobs. Many of these organizations offer forms, information, and other resources to help you start your business.

Here are a few of the most recognized organizations and associations:

- Pet Sit USA: **www.petsitusa.com**
- Pet Sitters International (PSI): **www.petsit.com**
- National Association of Professional Pet Sitters (NAPPS): **www.petsitters.org**
- Professional United Pet Sitters LLC (PUPS): **www.petsits.com**

In addition to pet sitting organizations, there are many associations in the United States that support animal lovers. By belonging to these groups, you will hone your animal care skills and remain up-to-date on the latest issues and techniques in pet care. Even if the group has membership qualifications that you do not match, but you can donate to the organizations and ask them for helpful literature and resources. You may learn about unfamiliar animals that will widen the scope of pets that you can care for. When you can tell your clients that you are a member of nationally recognized organizations that care for animals, you distinguish yourself from other sitters by portraying yourself as a leader in animal care.

Some of the best organizations for animal care include:

- The Humane Society of the United States
- The American Society for the Prevention of Cruelty to Animals
- Animal Charities of America
- Best Friends Animal Society

- American Partnership for Pets
- Save-A-Pet

Finally, there are organizations for business owners to help new businesses and support the small business world. As I mentioned earlier, the Better Business Bureau is an oversight organization that ensures excellence in business. By following the guidelines to become listed with the Bureau, your company becomes more credible. Another useful association is your local Chamber of Commerce. During my first year of business, I joined my county's Chamber and received many jobs through that association. Most Chambers offer frequent seminars, job fairs, and charity events that help business owners learn more about managing a business and help others to hear about your work. Membership fees are small and can include free advertising, member-to-member discounts, and business resources.

Case Study: Stephanie Erway

Stephanie Erway

Furr Pet's Sake, Inc.

Denver, Colorado

Building your business takes time and legwork. Promote your business through your local veterinarians and pet stores. Get to know them, and they will get to know you.

Spend time at their clinics and find out what type of veterinary care they provide. Use their services when needed. Ask to put your brochures or business cards in their business. Hand out business cards at local dog parks and dog or cat shows. Post door hangers to promote your business in areas you want to be in. The best way is to save the money and advertise in the local yellow pages. I also have a Web site that gives clients as much information as possible. I make sure organizations that promote pets/services have my Web site address. I reciprocate by linking to Web sites and putting their links on my Web site. I also belong to the clearing houses of pet sitting companies: Pet Sitters International and National Association of Professional Pet Sitters. Check locally and become a member of the Chamber of Commerce and Better Business Bureau. Network like crazy with women's networking groups. Do not be afraid to talk to people wherever you are.

Public Relations

Your image to the public should reflect your style, your business, and your love of animals. It is not enough to advertise your business; you need to get out in the community and gain recognition for yourself as a professional. You do this through public relations work, which results in free advertising for your business.

There are many ways to get involved, some of which may take more of your time as a pet sitter than you can afford. You may consider sponsoring a local charity (especially if it is animal-related), volunteer your time at animal hospitals or shelters, march in city parades, speak at non-profit or civic events, have a pet demonstration at a school, or sponsor a sports team. By doing this, you are telling your community that you value your neighborhood, and want to make a difference. You will likely gain pleasure from these activities, and the effort you put into these events will gain attention and goodwill from your town.

Another way to gain publicity is to write a newsletter or a column for a local newspaper. If you have writing skills, this is a way to get your business noticed. Local newspaper editors need a constant supply of news, and you can translate your love of animals into a helpful source of pet care information. If you produce your own newsletters, contact the owners of pet stores, feed supply companies, vets, animal hospitals, and shelters to distribute your material. You can also send a monthly newsletter to all your current clients. This keeps your name fresh in their minds. A newsletter might have photos of pets you care for, stories about animals, seasonal care tips, sitter profiles, ideas for activities or playing with pets, and more.

If you decide to create your own newsletter, there are several inexpensive software applications that can help you design and print a professional-looking publication, along with addressed envelopes or mailing labels. If you have a large mailing, check with the post office about getting bulk-rate postage to save money.

Another information-rich option is producing a monthly e-mail newsletter. This costs virtually nothing to produce, other than your time, and can be more welcome to people who are trying to reduce the amount of paper they receive and who appreciate receiving e-mail. You can collect e-mail addresses from your clients, friends, and people that you meet while talking about your business. Be careful about who you send the e-mail to, though. Some e-mail systems automatically mark such mail as "spam." Anti-spam laws are becoming more strict, so be sure the person truly wants your e-mail before sending it. You should always disclose who you are as the sender, and you also want to have some way for the recipient to be able to "opt-out" of you e-mail list. You can read more about spam laws at **www.ftc.gov**.

Though many people are nervous or even terrified to speak in public, giving a talk in public can become less frightening as you get used to it. If you are able to give a speech to clubs, associations, and civic groups, you will increase your client base. That may be worth the butterflies in the stomach and the sweaty palms.

If you are going the public-speaking route, start small. Get some time with a mother's group or a group of friends. Encourage the group to stop you and ask questions, since this will break up the flow a bit and help you feel like you are having a natural conversation. You will find after a few talks that people appreciate your expert advice, and this will give you the confidence you need to approach larger groups. If you belong to a professional organization, you will hear other speakers and learn from their talks. When it is your turn to give a speech, they will probably give you the same attention and consideration that you gave them.

You can also come up with your own public-relations event and have some fun as well. During summer town festivals or winter parties, host a doggie dress-up or costume party. This may be fun at Halloween as well. Some churches hold an annual animal-blessing ceremony; offer your time to photograph the animals or work out a plan with a local veterinarian to provide microchip implants for the animals. During the holidays, send each of your clients a Christmas or Hanukkah card. Encourage local businesses to participate in the annual Take Our Pets to Work Day.

"A dog is the only thing on earth that loves you more than he loves himself."

~Josh Billings

Managing Your Clients

A new client calls. She mentions she saw your flyer in her veterinarian's clinic and is interested in having you care for her cat and dog. Write a note in your marketing file on which flyer and which office brought you this client. This is valuable information for your promotional efforts. Next, check your schedule for availability on the dates she needs a sitter. Make sure the location of the house is in the area you serve. Ask a few questions about the types of services she needs, and confirm that you perform all those tasks. After responding to her questions about rates and activities, she wants to hire you. At this point, set up a client meeting.

Dress professionally and conservatively to meet with your client. This does not mean that you arrive for your interview in a business suit or high heels; you do not want to give the client the impression that you would not hug a dog or allow a cat to jump up on your lap. The appropriate attire for this type of meeting is business casual — something nicer than a pair of jeans and a sweatshirt but less formal than panty hose or a tie. Try nice casual pants and a buttoned shirt.

If you can, try to arrive ten minutes early for your appointment. While the client may not care that you are early for an interview, it will register with them that you plan ahead and can be counted on to show up early. This will be much more important to them when they imagine that you will be early to let their dog out when it needs to relieve itself.

Projecting confidence and professionalism is important, especially if you feel less comfortable around humans than around pets. If you are nervous, practice a basic interview with a friend or your spouse until you feel prepared. Before the interview, remind yourself that you know your business, you love animals, and you have the experience to nurture this client's furry friends. They will sense this reassurance from you.

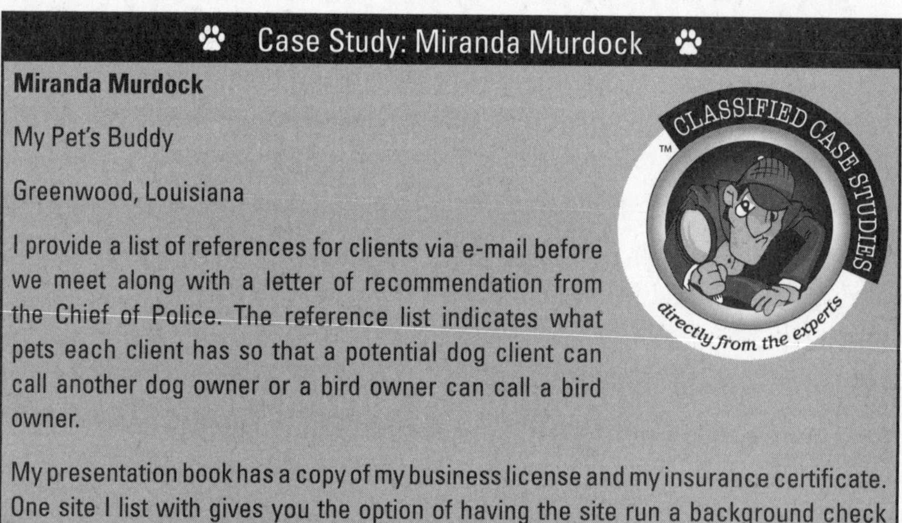

Case Study: Miranda Murdock

Miranda Murdock

My Pet's Buddy

Greenwood, Louisiana

I provide a list of references for clients via e-mail before we meet along with a letter of recommendation from the Chief of Police. The reference list indicates what pets each client has so that a potential dog client can call another dog owner or a bird owner can call a bird owner.

My presentation book has a copy of my business license and my insurance certificate. One site I list with gives you the option of having the site run a background check on you, and then it is available to their member, and I did that. During the meet and greet I explain my policies meant to protect them. They know I understand the trust they are placing in me.

The Client Interview

The first time you meet with a client, each of you are interviewing the other to be sure this will be a satisfactory partnership. You want to be sure the client has reasonable expectations and will work with you for the pet's good. The client will need to know they can trust you to love and nurture their pet as they would. While some sitters charge a small fee for this meeting, others include it as part of the service.

Your prospective client will want to know about your business practices and policies. Tell the client your office hours. Provide contact information and explain how soon they can expect a response. Clients will be reassured to know that you keep regular office hours and that an answering machine or service will handle calls when you are out. Even more important, they will get your cell phone number, and you have set the expectation of a call back within 24 hours.

Let the client know how much notice you will need to care for their pets. A two-week time is reasonable, but you may request more advance notice around busy times such as holidays, when bookings may fill up fast. If you can handle short-notice bookings, tell them so, but do not provide assurance that you can handle last-minute calls unless you are positive you can accommodate them. Let them know if there is an additional charge for short-notice assignments.

Over the phone or in company literature you may have quoted your established fees. These should cover the most common pet care requests, while indicating that fees for special services are determined on a case-by-case basis. Now is the time to review these rates and discuss how any special requests may change what you charge. By the end of the visit, you and the client should have an agreed-upon final cost for the assignment and a mutual understanding of what is expected of you. You should also discuss when you expect payment, whether a deposit is required, and what methods of payment (check, credit card, and PayPal) you accept.

Show the client your credentials. Give them proof of your bonding and insurance coverage. Discuss your experience and certifications or accreditations. Show the client you are supremely qualified to care for their pets. Provide them with pre-qualified references.

The client must know that you have contingency plans in place for any type of problem. You should discuss procedures such as your plan for inclement weather or illness, how you will care for sick or injured pets, and your disaster preparedness plan. If another sitter or partner will take over services if you are incapacitated or if you employ several sitters for your business, tell the client about the people, their qualifications, and their experience. Reassure the client about your procedures for protecting their information and keeping access to their homes secure. Finally, you should discuss how you will handle problems in the home, ranging from pet accidents to a broken furnace. The step-by-step procedures found in Chapter 5 will produce excellent talking points for this discussion.

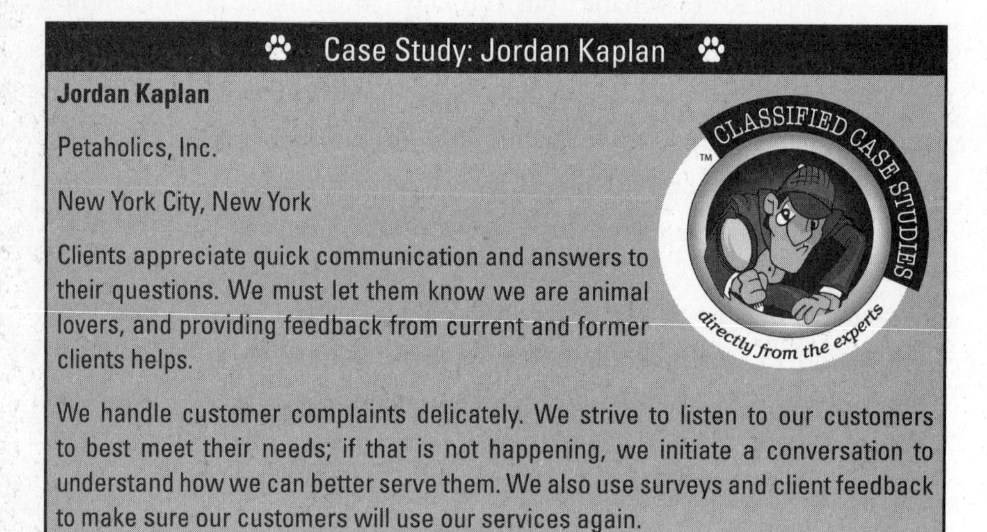

Case Study: Jordan Kaplan

Jordan Kaplan

Petaholics, Inc.

New York City, New York

Clients appreciate quick communication and answers to their questions. We must let them know we are animal lovers, and providing feedback from current and former clients helps.

We handle customer complaints delicately. We strive to listen to our customers to best meet their needs; if that is not happening, we initiate a conversation to understand how we can better serve them. We also use surveys and client feedback to make sure our customers will use our services again.

After you have discussed what the client can expect from you, it is time for the client to understand your expectations. These expectations are vital for you to give their pets the care they deserve. If a client balks about these requests, this pet care situation may not be right for your business. You may want to leave the following checklist of requests for the client (as included on the companion CD-ROM):

- Provide documentation confirming that your pet is up-to-date on its shots. Make sure your pet wears current vaccination tags on its collar.

- If your pet chews on things, set out "chew toys" and do whatever is necessary to protect your personal items and home furnishings from his teeth while you are away.
- Write out your pet's favorite hiding places. This helps the sitter find your pet if he or she does not appear when the sitter arrives.
- If your pet has any unusual habits, like destructive behavior when left alone, change in bowel or eating habits, or other problems, tell your sitter about these in advance.
- If you own dogs and cats, please note that the sitter is honor-bound to care for the cats as well. Please do not ask the sitter to ignore the cat in return for a lower rate.
- Set out everything your pet needs in one visible and accessible area. This includes food, treats, food and water bowls, medications, leash, can opener, toys, cleaning supplies, litter and scoop, pet towels, house-breaking materials, watering can for plants, and anything else needed to accomplish the agreed-upon work.
- Provide extra food, litter, and supplies just in case you are home later than expected.
- Be sure to leave plastic bags for sanitary disposal of feces.
- Do not expect your sitter to pick up any pet messes that accumulated before their contract period.
- Clean out your refrigerator so that food does not spoil, and wash all dishes so that there is no chance of ants or other pests invading the house.

- Make sure the sitter knows how to operate your heat and air conditioner, and which settings should be used for the comfort of your pet. Check your settings before you leave.

- Close off any areas of your home that are off limits to the pet or sitter, and let them know about it in advance. If there are any particular problems they should be aware of, such as a leaky faucet or a cat that likes to get into the garbage, tell them before you leave.

- If you are leaving anything specifically for your pet sitter, such as a batch of cookies or a tip, leave them a note. Sitters will not take anything from a house unless they are specifically invited to do so.

- If other people may access the house or care for the pets, make sure the sitter knows what they are responsible for and who they might encounter in the house. The sitter will not automatically know the difference between an authorized house visit and a break-in.

- Notify your veterinarian in writing that a pet sitter will be caring for your pet, and authorize the veterinarian to extend medical care during your absence if it becomes necessary.

Case Study: Miranda Murdock

Miranda Murdock

My Pet's Buddy

Greenwood, LA

CLASSIFIED CASE STUDIES™ directly from the experts

I recently had a visit where I could not get the dog to go back into the "dog" room — the area where they were kept when there are no humans present. The dog ran from room to room, hid under furniture, and attempted to bite me when I reached for her. I decided to leave her where she was because I cannot care for any animals if I am injured.

Case Study: Miranda Murdock

I left a note on the counter explaining what happened, posted a note on the front and back door so the owner would not be surprised when they walked in or the dog tried to race out, and also left a voice mail on the client's cell phone just in case it was dark when they got home and they could not see the note. I think clients are more forgiving when they are not surprised.

During the interview, get to know the pet and allow it time to adjust to you. Do not allow the owner to force the pet to like you. Some pets are shy and cannot be expected to warm up to a stranger immediately. Dogs take their cues from their owners and will need a few minutes to sniff you and read your body language before approaching you or allowing you to touch them. Do not force this initial greeting because you may cause long-lasting damage to your relationship with the pet. Always allow a dog to sniff your hand before raising it over them to pet their heads.

The client interview is a time when you must use all your powers of observation. Observe the pet's behavior and its response to its owners. This will give you clues to how the animal will expect to be treated by you. Does the dog seem territorial, or does he tend to bark? Does he seem friendly, or do you see any signs of aggression? You must be on the lookout for warning signals that tell you this may be a bad sitting situation, or that you may have trouble with this pet. You should also look for clues that tell you the pet's normal behavior. If you visit the pet later and he or she acts differently from what you first observed, it may not be just loneliness; there may be something else wrong.

Observe how the client handles and pets their animals. Do they hug? Do they pick up their cats? Do they seem to scratch the dog in a particular place? While you are there, give it a try. Mimic the owner's care. This may help the animal feel comfortable with you, as well as give the animal added comfort while their primary care giver is away. However, always watch the animal's signs while you are petting them to be sure they are not alarmed or uncomfortable. Many animals will only allow you to pet their stomachs after they have developed a comfort level with you. Laid-back ears, a whipping tail, and narrowed eyes may be telling you to stop.

This is also the time to observe your potential client and your surroundings. Do you see any red flags, such as a filthy home, mistreated or frightened animals, or neglect? Contact the Humane Society or a veterinarian if you have major concerns. Is the neighborhood one that you would feel comfortable walking a pet around at night, or entering or exiting your car when it is dark? Do you feel comfortable around the client, or do you have concerns? Does the person seem reasonable and trustworthy? Pay attention to what your instincts tell you. Your instincts may be right.

If you and the client seem to click and the situation seems right, have the client complete pet information forms and sign a contract. Give the client one copy of the contract. Sample contract and pet information sheets are shown below and are available on the companion CD-ROM. A valid contract should state exactly what pets, services, and dates are covered for the quoted rate.

(Company Name) Pet Sitting Service Contract

Contact Information

Note: If something does not apply to you or your home, please indicate by entering "N/A" in the space.

Name: ______________________________

E-mail address: ______________________________

Home Phone: ______________________________

Business Phone: ______________________________

Address: ______________________________

Who else has access to your home? Please write name and phone numbers.

Your Landlord: ______________________________

Maid/Cleaning Service: ______________________________

(Company Name) Pet Sitting Service Contract

Other: ______________________________

Describe Your Pet(s)

If you have more than three pets, please attach additional information at bottom of sheet.

Pet's Name and species:

1) ____________ 2) ____________ 3) ____________

Sex:

1) ____________ 2) ____________ 3) ____________

Favorite toys/treats:

1) ____________ 2) ____________ 3) ____________

Number of visits per day: ______________________________

Sample Pet Information Form

Owner's name: ______________________________

Home #: ______________________________

Cell #: ______________________________

Work #: ______________________________

Address: ______________________________

Designated Emergency Pet Guardian:

Home #: ______________________________

Cell #: ______________________________

Work #: ______________________________

E-mail address: ______________________________

Address: ______________________________

Pet's name: ______________________________

Dog Cat Other (circle one)

Sample Pet Information Form

Breed: ______________________________

Sex: Male Female

Age: ______________________________

Spayed/Neutered: Yes No

County Tag ID: ______________________________

ID Microchip: Yes No

If yes, Microchip #: ______________________________

Weight: ______________________________

Height: ______________________________

Eye color: ______________________________

Tail: ______________________________

Hair color: ______________________________

Hair length: ______________________________

Veterinarian's office: ______________________________

Veterinarian's name: ______________________________

Veterinarian's Phone #: ______________________________

Date of last vaccinations: ______________________________

Any medical conditions/allergies? ______________________________

Any special medications? ______________________________

General disposition: ______________________________

Is your pet good around children? Yes No

Is your pet good around dogs? Yes No

Is your pet good around cats? Yes No

Specific identifying marks and/or features that would help to identify your pet: _

____

Sample Pet Information Form

Names of people who could identify your pet:

1. Name ______________________________

   Phone: ______________________________

2. Name ______________________________

   Phone: ______________________________

General Pet Care Information

PLEASE NOTE: Care will be given in watching both your pet(s) and your home. However, due to the unpredictable nature of animals, we cannot accept responsibility for any mishaps of an extraordinary or unusual nature (i.e., biting, furniture damage, accidental death or extraordinary occurrence) or any complications in administering medications to the animal. Nor can we be liable for injury, disappearance, death or fines of pet(s) with access to the outdoors.

Veterinarian Preference: ______________________________

Phone: ______________________________

Are pets secured in home or yard?: ______________________________

Terms and Conditions

Please fill in all blanks and read carefully.

1. The parties herein agree as follows: The initial term of this contract shall be from ______________________________through______________________________. In the event of early return home, client must notify pet sitter promptly to avoid being charged for unnecessary visits(s).

2. The baseline fee is (cost per visit) x (number of visits) for a total of ______________________________Other fees for additional services or circumstances may apply. Any additional visits made or services performed shall be paid for at the agreed contract rate. Pet sitter is authorized to perform care and services as outlined on this contract. Pet sitter is also authorized by Client (name entered below) to seek emergency veterinary care with release from all liabilities related to transportation, treatment, and expense.

3. Should specified veterinarian be unavailable, pet sitter is authorized to approve medical and/or emergency treatment (excluding euthanasia) as recommended

Sample Pet Information Form

by a veterinarian. Client agrees to reimburse pet sitter/company for expenses incurred, plus any additional fee for attending to this need and any expenses incurred for any other home/food/supplies needed.

4. In the event of inclement weather or natural disaster, pet sitter is entrusted to use best judgment in caring for pet(s) and home. Pet sitter/company will be held harmless for consequences related to such decisions.

5. Pet sitter agrees to provide the services stated in this contract in a reliable, caring and trustworthy manner. In consideration of these services and as an express condition thereof, the client expressly waives and relinquishes any and all claims against said pet sitter/company except those arising from negligence or willful misconduct the part of the sitter/company.

6. Client understands this contract also serves as an invoice and takes full responsibility for prompt payment of fees upon completion of services contracted. A finance charge of ___percent per month will be added to unpaid balances after thirty (30) days. A handling fee ($20) will be charged on all returned checks. One half deposit is required on lengthy assignments, and first-time clients or clients with a history of late payment will be required to pay in advance before services are rendered. In the event it is necessary to initiate collection proceedings on the account, client will be responsible for all attorney's fees and costs of collection.

7. In the event of personal emergency or illness of pet sitter, Client authorizes pet sitter to arrange for another qualified person to fulfill responsibilities as set forth in this contract. Client will be notified in such a case.

8. All pets are to be currently vaccinated. Should pet sitter be bitten or otherwise exposed to any disease or ailment received from Client's animal which has not been properly and currently vaccinated, it will be the client's responsibility to pay all costs and damages incurred by the victim.

9. Pet sitter/company reserves the right to terminate this contract at any time before or during its term. If pet sitter/company, in its sole discretion, determines that Client's pet poses a danger to health or safety of pet sitter, if concerns prohibit pet sitter from caring for pet, Client authorizes pet to be placed in a kennel, with all charges therefrom charged to Client.

10. Client authorizes this signed contract to be valid approval for future services of any purpose provided by this contract permitting pet sitter/company to accept telephone reservations for service and enter premises without additional signed contracts or written authorization.

Sample Pet Information Form

I have reviewed this Service Contract for accuracy and understand the contents of this form.

Date: ______________________________

Client: ______________________________

Pet Sitter/Company: ______________________________

Before you leave the interview, collect the keys and try them at the door. You do not want to be stuck with a key that does not work and a pet that needs attention when the owner is gone. If the owner will have you enter the house through a keypad entry, try the code before you leave. Make sure they give you details on how to disarm an alarm or security system. Do not allow them to just give you a garage door opener or rely on a system connected to house power. If there is a power outage in the neighborhood, you are locked out. It is also a good idea to persuade the owner to leave a key in a hidden area around the house, in case all else fails.

Case Study: Terri Randall

Terri Randall

Creature Comforts Pet Care

Sheridan, Wyoming

CLASSIFIED CASE STUDIES™ directly from the experts

How you answer potential client's initial calls can make all the difference. Regardless of whether I am in a hurry or what kind of day I am having, I smile as I talk to the person and believe that comes across in my voice. I engage them, ask about their pets, and make them feel at ease. I offer a number of references from happy clients as well as local area veterinarians. I then set up the consultation where I meet with the client and their pets in their home.

How you conduct those first meetings is crucial. I do not have one set way; I get a good feel for what type of person it is over the phone and act accordingly. Some

Case Study: Terri Randall

people are more business-like, and some are folksier. You have to know what type of person you are dealing with. The same holds true for the pets. There is no one-size-fits-all in this business.

Good Customer Service

Now that you have a client, or a list of clients, there are things you should do to make sure you maintain the client relationship. There are tools to keeping a customer happy — tools appropriate to any service relationship. Good customer service is key to keeping clients coming back for more.

Always make a good impression. While you may dress in a casual fashion to take care of the pets, take care not to look sloppy. If your company name is on the side of your car and you jump out in torn, stained clothes or act unprofessionally, you are giving your company a bad name without saying a word. If someone calls your business, make sure there is a businesslike message on the answering machine or your voice mail; do not try something whimsical or cute. You want to give the impression that you are a solid, dependable person.

Part of good customer service is the focus that you give each client. When you are working with that client, focus on the job at hand. When you meet with the client, do not discuss the specifics of any other client unless it relates to how you are especially qualified to handle this client's pet. Whether you are with a client or taking care of a pet, focus on that job, and do not allow your attention to wander. Do not make or return calls unless they are emergencies.

You should be accessible to your clients. They should know how to contact you, and when they can expect a return call. Always return your calls promptly. It is anxiety-producing than being away from home in an emergency and being unable to reach the sitter caring for your pets. If the return call will take some time, and you have to put it off until later, at least call the person and tell them you received their message. Let them know when you will be available for a longer discussion. This lets your clients know that you care about them, their business, and their animals.

Make sure you have answers to clients' questions and concerns. You may not know everything about every single aspect of pet sitting, but you should have good responses to common questions. If you do not know the answer, do not just say, "I do not know." Say, "I am not sure, but I will find out." Make sure you follow up with the answer. If a client asks, for example, if you know how to administer fluids to a cat with kidney disease, you may be stumped. But unless you know you could not possibly do it, ask the client to teach you, and willingly work at it. By showing you are teachable, the client will have more confidence in your ability to handle situations requiring flexibility.

The extras that you offer you clients are what will set you apart from other sitters and will define your personal style in caring for animals. More than just the services you offer are the extras that show people you care about them and their animals. Never give clients the impression that you are "squeezing them in," doing them a favor, or that your care is a pure business proposition. Communicate your love and enthusiasm for animals. There are ways to go that extra mile to make the assignment even more positive for the owner and yourself. Successful sitters have offered the following extra services:

- Taking photos of the animal during appointments with a digital camera or Polaroid

- Sending sympathy cards when hearing that a cared-for pet has passed away

- Updating a Web site daily or sending an e-mail with news of the pet's visit

- Writing a newsletter on pet care and animal lovers' topics
- Clipping coupons for the brand of food that an animal eats and leaving it at the home
- Providing a special toy for the pet

Case Study: Janet Dill

Janet Dill

The Pet Nanny

Gurnee, Illinois

I am a part-time sitter, and I specialize in overnight visits where I stay with the animal through the night. To make sure my customers use my service again, I provide reliable service and a daily report card.

I usually do a bit extra, like "poop scoop" the yard, pick up mail, handle the bins on garbage day, provide training exercises upon request, and give exercise time, not just walking, if the pet is able. I ensure everything is the way they left it, and leave a treat/toy and a photo for the client with a welcome home note or card. For special occasions, I have left flowers with a note from their pets. Any special consideration lets the client know that you went an extra step.

Difficult Clients

Any time we deal with other human beings, there is potential for difficult situations to arise. This is especially true in a pet sitting arrangement, when people are emotionally involved with their pets. While dealing with difficult clients, it is important to not take the behavior or situation personally. You should also deal with the situation logically, unemotionally, and with a view to good customer service and what is best for the business.

One troublesome area is clients who tend to take up a large amount of your time. These clients may be new to having someone care for their pets, they may be unsure about you, or they may just be over-involved in their pet's life. At first, you may want to put in the extra time to reassure your client, but if you are spending several hours a day on the phone telling the client about his dog's play habits or analyzing its bowel movements, you are taking time away from other clients. The situation may not be cost-effective.

There are several solutions for such a problem. You can take control of the situation and set boundaries. Let the owner know that you have dedicated only 15 minutes to consultations with him, and firmly manage the conversation while talking to him. If the person is just talkative, consistently guide him back to the topic at hand. If the conversations continue to run longer, tell the owner that you will charge an additional rate for these extra discussions.

Another troublesome area is the client that expects you to shred carrots into the dog bowl, meet the repairman, and wash Fido's blankets every day. Extra services may be acceptable if covered in a contract and in your fees, but a client that springs these on you at the last minute may not have paid for the service. Do not do than you were hired to do. Stand firm and decline the extra duties unless you have the time and they are willing to pay. You are a businessperson, not a servant. If emergencies come up, such as a rush visit to the veterinarian or an emergency air conditioner repair, you should talk to the client about how this will affect their bill. If too many emergencies or last-minute favors come up, address it directly with the client and bring it to an end.

People who love animals enough to hire a pet sitter are not the types to write bad checks or avoid paying for services, but sometimes you will have to deal with a delinquent account. Start by placing a pay envelope on the table or counter on your last visit. A friendly reminder letter or phone call may be enough to bring the client up-to-date. If you do not receive payment, contact the client to see if there are unusual circumstances causing delinquency. You might need to work out other payment arrangements. If all else fails, you may need to contact a lawyer and discontinue services to that customer. See the operating procedures chapter of this book for more information on how to handle delinquent accounts.

The Sitting Appointment

Each of the previous sections has led us to the fun part of your job: the actual sitting appointment. This section will walk through the basic sitting services. In Chapters 8 and 9 we will explore specialized care. Your pet sitting services should reflect your personal style and love for animals. Pet sitting is a detail-oriented job that requires you to be on your toes while caring for other peoples' animals. After you get into a daily routine, it will be easy to remember each step of the process.

Dress for your day in professional-looking but comfortable clothing, such as jeans or khaki pants with a sweater or a nice T-shirt. You might consider having shirts made with your company logo or name on them. Make sure you are not wearing anything that would be irreplaceable or hard to clean. Always wear comfortable shoes; your feet will thank you.

Before you leave, or the night before, prepare your service kit. This should contain your business cards and company flyers, each of the pet information forms for the day's appointments, and envelopes to leave with clients so they can mail payment. Also include a pad of paper for leaving notes for the client, each client's keys, and a daily report sheet. The daily report is a log of mileage, client names and addresses, times of arrival and departure at each home, and any notes about the visits. You will use this information later to help with billing and, if needed, resolving any issues that may arise.

If you stock your car with the tools you may need for your services, you will be prepared for surprises and emergencies. You may want to keep the following items available:

- A spare leash
- An animal carrier
- Gloves
- A "pooper scooper"
- A scrub brush and a container of carpet cleaner
- A whisk broom and dustpan
- A flashlight
- Area maps

When you arrive at the client's home, check the area to be sure things look safe and that there are no signs of intrusion or damage. Write down your mileage in the log, and grab your equipment and sitting kit. Pick up any mail and newspapers on your way in, or pick that up later when you have had a chance to take care of the animals.

Case Study: Jordan Kaplan

Jordan Kaplan

Petaholics

New York City, New York

CLASSIFIED CASE STUDIES™ directly from the experts

To ensure your safety during pet sitting appointments, always stay alert when entering a home or meeting a new animal; you never know how a pet will react.

Show the animal confidence and always let a pet get comfortable with you first. If you understand different breeds and their drives, you will be more successful in caring for them. Pets give signals before a reaction occurs. Watch their body language for clues.

Some pets are eager to run out the door as soon as someone opens it. Try to block the door with your body or bag to be sure you do not lose them the minute the door opens. After you are inside, make sure you put the key in a pocket or on a wristband around your arm so that you do not misplace it or forget it until after you have closed the door.

Find each of the animals and make sure they are all in good health. Then check the house for accidents, problems, messes, or dangerous conditions. You may find a leaky toilet or an iron that has been left on. While you are checking all the rooms, let the dogs out into the yard if it is fenced, or place them on a chain so they can have a potty break.

Next, wash the pets' food and water bowls, and refill them according to the owner's directions. Follow the instructions precisely, unless you fear there is an element of neglect or insufficient feeding in the instructions. Many animals are sensitive to changes in diet or routine; it is wise to take care of them just as their owners would. If you are sitting for small animals such as rodents, reptiles, birds, or fish, remember that these animals are sensitive to fluctuations in temperature and moisture. Check the cage or aquarium to be sure that the settings are optimal for the animal's health. If you are caring for cats, clean the litter box and change the litter before the cat refuses to use a dirty box.

While you are performing these chores, talk to the animals. They are likely to be lonely without their owners around, and will appreciate human interaction. When the animals are eating, use your time to water plants, sort the mail, and take care of any other tasks in your contract. If there are any messes to clean up, or accidents such as a plant knocked over or a chewed-up shoe, take care of those problems and note it in your log. You may have to explain these things to the owner when he or she returns.

Pets need love, attention, exercise, and grooming just as much as they need food and water. The remainder of your appointment should be devoted to these tasks. The owner may ask you to take the dog for walks, or let him loose in the yard or the dog park. A cat may need brushing, petting, or play time with toys. The owner might like you to let the reptile or bird loose from the cage for some free exercise. If you are sitting for exotic pets, make sure you understand the limitations and behaviors of the animals before letting them loose. Animals can be unpredictable.

If you are watching barnyard animals or livestock, the routine will be similar. Horses will need some grooming and exercise, which can take the form of letting the horse loose in a paddock or pasture, or running them on a lunge line, where you stand stationary while the horse runs. Some livestock have tricky digestive systems, such as horses, sheep, and goats. Again, be sure to precisely follow the owner's instructions. When caring for livestock, double-check gates and fences before you set them free.

Make sure that when you leave there are no toys or other objects left out that the animals can choke on, chew up, or destroy. Check the service agreement or contract one last time to be sure you have done everything expected of you. Write a note to the client telling him or her about your visit. Owners especially like to hear about cute or interesting things that their pet does while they are gone. This makes them feel a little closer to the animal when they cannot see it. If this is your last visit, you may want to leave a stamped envelope and an invoice for your services. Finally, check all the animals one last time to be sure they are where they belong and that they seem healthy. Check one last time to ensure you have your paperwork, keys, and belongings before you leave.

Case Study: Janet Dill

Janet Dill

The Pet Nanny

Gurnee, Illinois

When you are caring for animals, always be mindful of your surroundings and anything suspicious. Keep your cell phone with you at all times and have emergency and contacts numbers programmed in it.

Do not advertise your pet sit business on your vehicle when you visit clients' homes. This tells everyone the client is not home. Never enter a home that appears to have been broken into. Always carry your pet sit contract with you in case you have to explain your presence.

Sitting Appointment Do's and Don'ts

Do's

1. Check that each of the animals is present and healthy when you arrive for the appointment, and double-check that each animal is present and in its proper place (cage, aquarium, living room) before leaving the home.

2. Provide extra cool, clean water in the summertime.

3. Follow the feeding instructions exactly. Make sure you understand instructions such as whether the dog has canned food mixed with its dry food, or if these are served separately. An animal may not touch its food if it is not served in the usual place or prepared in the usual manner.

4. Be firm but loving in establishing rules of behavior. You are the master of the situation.

5. Wipe off a dog's paws when it comes in out of the snow or ice. Watch for salt and other chemicals which can hurt its foot pads.

6. Be aware of how the pets interact if you are caring for multiple pets.

7. Keep a pet carrier in your car in case you need to transport a sick animal to the hospital.

8. Be careful when handling large pets, especially more than one at a time. It can be easy to get tangled up in leashes or halters, and break something in the home or hurt yourself.

9. Make sure you turn off all water faucets and appliances before leaving the home.

10. Contact the client when you have pet sitting problems — they will want to be informed, even if they cannot do anything about the problem.

11. Make sure the temperature of the house and the cage/aquarium are correct before leaving the appointment.

12. Clean up any animal messes promptly with cleaning materials that are safe for the surface you are cleaning.

13. Keep your clients' house keys safe on your person at all times.

14. Ring the client's doorbell before entering the home, in case the client returned home early.

15. Carry with you identification that describes you as a professional pet sitter, and information about an emergency contact to care for the animals if you are incapacitated.

Don'ts

1. Do not take children or friends on pet sitting appointments. Your insurance will not cover their injuries or accidental damage.

2. Do not give animals any kind of medication without the permission of the owner or instruction of a veterinarian.

3. Do not discuss a client's travel plans or their personal information over a cell phone or cordless phone since this information can be picked up by others.

4. Do not accept a garage door opener or door code in lieu of a key. If the power goes out, you will not be able to enter the home.

5. Do not leave collected mail in a place that can be seen from a window. This is a clear indication that the owners are not home.

6. Do not let a dog off the leash during a snowstorm. It cannot easily retrace its scent over snow or ice and could get lost.

7. Do not use the client's swimming pool, exercise equipment, phone, computer, or electronics unless you have their permission.

8. Do not give the animals extra treats or special foods against the owner's instructions, even if you want to pamper them a little. The animal could have a strict diet or may be allergic or sensitive to food changes.

9. Do not force a dog to run in hot or humid weather.

10. Do not leave out any sources of food, even if the client says that the animal will not get into the food bag. Many animals will gorge

themselves on a food supply. Also make sure any human food is out-of-reach.

11. Do not let strangers pet the animals in your care while walking or exercising them. If the animal is hurt or hurts the stranger, you are liable.

12. Do not let a pet out of the cage unless the owner has indicated it is all right to do so. If you do let it out, make sure you know how to catch it and return it to its cage — and where it tends to hide if it does not want to be caught!

Sitter Safety

Sitters should always exercise caution on a sitting appointment. As for any other service person that must go into a stranger's home, walk down dark or deserted streets, or enter unfamiliar neighborhoods, there are risks involved with the pet sitting job. Pet sitters should be aware of their surroundings and listen to the "gut feel" of a situation. If a situation appears dangerous, get out.

Here are other ideas to help keep you safe while caring for animals:

- Always carry a cell phone with you, or know where the nearest pay phone or friendly neighbor is located.

- Develop a distress code with your family, employees, or backup sitters — one that sounds like an innocent message but that your team will understand as an alert. If you are in a trouble situation, you can communicate that something is wrong while appearing to leave a neutral message.

- When you initially meet with a client, tell a friend, employee, or family member the details of the visit and ask them to call your cell phone during the meeting. If there is a problem or you are in a dangerous situation, you can alert them with your distress code.

- If you feel uneasy about a visit to a particular area, ask a friend to go with you.

- As you go from appointment to appointment, leave messages on the business answering machine about the arrival and departure times and which stop will be next. These updates will help people retrace your steps if there is a problem — or if they need to determine where you are going next.

- If you see any suspicious cars, people, or activity in a neighborhood, report it to the police immediately. Ask your client who else has access to the home, and find out what kind of car any other visitors might drive.

- When you arrive for an appointment, scan the area for potential danger. Do not exit your car if you suspect trouble.

- Keep your car doors locked at each visit, and hold your house or car keys ready in your hand when you enter the home or walk to your car.

- Consider carrying safety items such as a whistle, air horn, mace, or pepper spray, according to local and state laws. Keep these items close at hand and be sure you know how to use them.

- During your daytime visits, turn on a porch or outdoor light so that when you return for an evening visit you can enter the home in the light.

- When you enter the home, call the animal by name to reassure it that you are a friendly, known human. This may also scare away a burglar that could be in the house.

- Pay attention to a dog's body language. If you are walking a dog and its ears go up or its tail stops wagging, this can be a warning to you. If you see signs of aggression in the dog, do not approach it any further.

Sitter safety includes caring for your own health. If you are not healthy, you can transmit illness to a pet or catch an illness from a pet. You will not be able to offer your best to the animals in your care if you are not well. Make sure you wash your hands thoroughly with antibacterial soap after each appointment. Keep a special pair of boots in your vehicle that you use only for barn appointments.

If you find that an animal you are caring for has fleas or mites, be sure to spray yourself down so that you do not carry an infestation into someone else's home. Pregnant women should not handle a cat's litter box, due to the danger of contracting toxoplasmosis, an internal parasite, from the cat's feces.

The tasks of pet sitting can take a toll on your body. Make sure you get plenty of rest and sufficient exercise to keep up with your four-footed charges. Maintaining a positive mental attitude and developing healthy responses to stress will keep your immune system in better shape, as well as making your days more pleasant. Take care of yourself first so that you can take care of everything else you are responsible for.

"I love cats because I enjoy my home;
and little by little, they become its
visible soul."
~Jean Cocteau

Common Household Pets

When a client hires you to care for his or her animals, chances are you will be caring for dogs and cats and possibly a few other common household pets. This chapter gives basic information on caring for these animals, as well as tips and tricks from experts. While much of this may be a review for those with experience working with these pets, all should find some helpful information.

Case Study: Stephanie Erway

Stephanie Erway

Furr Pet's Sake, Inc.

Denver, Colorado

You must learn how to read the pets in your charge. Never walk into a house being afraid; animals will sense your fear.

Never just approach an animal. Let them come up to you. Do not bend over them, and do not just reach for an animal. Turn your palm up when offering it to a dog. Get down on their level by sitting down and allowing them to sniff you. You never know when a dog wagging its tail will turn on you. Cats — never ever reach for them, use a loud voice, or chase them to get to see them. Just sit down and allow the cat to check you out. If you put your hand down and the cat rubs against it, then it is all right to pet them. Be polite and not overbearing when dealing with cats. They do not care that much about you and prefer their owner over you. It takes time for cats to like you. I find having treats of either dried shrimp or dried fish are the easiest way to get the cats to like you.

Dogs

Dogs and humans have been friends for a long time. Scientists believe that dogs were domesticated between 12,000 and 25,000 years ago, and that all dogs evolved from the wolf. Today there are more than 400 breeds of dog, ranging in size from four-pound teacup poodles to Irish wolfhounds, whose three-foot stature earns them the title of tallest canine. The most popular dogs are the non-pedigreed mixed breeds.

Special breeds have special health issues. For example, Bulldogs tend to have respiratory problems due to the angle of their noses; the wrinkly skin of a Shar-Pei makes it more susceptible to skin rashes and pimples. It is important that you learn all you can about dog breeds so that you can look for the problems of a particular breed.

Dogs will likely be the most frequently-requested service of your pet sitting business. Be completely familiar with dog handling, feeding, and care. Though you are expected to follow the owner's wishes in caring for their dog, here are some guidelines to help you make common-sense decisions.

Feeding

- Puppies eight to 12 weeks old need four meals each day.
- Puppies three to six months old need three meals each day.
- Puppies six months to one year need two meals each day.
- When your dog reaches his first birthday, one meal each day is enough.
- For some dogs, including larger canines or those prone to bloat, it is better to provide two smaller meals.

Unlike cats and many other pets, you cannot leave extra food for dogs to nibble on throughout the day. Dogs will gorge themselves on any amount you give them. It is important to carefully monitor their food. If you are caring for two or more dogs in the same home, ask the client whether the dogs should be separated while they eat. One dog may require a special diet that the other dog should not eat — or one dog may gobble all of his food and then take the other dog's share. If the household has both dogs and cats, make sure you know the arrangement to keep the dog's food area separate from the cat's food area. Dogs will not discriminate between eating their food and the cat's food.

Even if the owner tells you the dog does not mind being approached while eating, keep your distance. Outside their normal routine, any animal can behave in unexpected ways. Find out the signals and words that the dog has been trained to obey: "Down!" or "Off!" when they jump on you; "Stay!" or an upheld hand when they should stay where they are. You are responsible for the dog's discipline while the owner is gone. Do not let him or her get into bad habits like jumping on visitors or sleeping on the couch if that is not normally allowed.

Premium-quality dry food provides a well-balanced diet for adult dogs and is often mixed with water, broth, or canned food. Some dogs may enjoy cottage cheese, cooked egg, or fruits and vegetables, and some pets prefer a baby carrot to a commercially-prepared dog treat.

Puppies should be fed a high-quality, brand-name puppy food. Do not give dogs "people food." It can result in vitamin and mineral imbalances, bone and teeth problems, picky eating habits, and potentially to obesity. Clean, fresh water should be available at all times, and food and water dishes should be washed frequently.

Exercise

Dogs need exercise to burn calories, stimulate their minds, and stay healthy. Exercise also tends to help dogs avoid boredom, which can lead to destructive behaviors. A big part of your job will be to organize walks and supervised fun and games to control the pet's instinctual urges to dig, herd, chew, retrieve and chase.

Individual exercise needs vary based on breed or breed mix, sex, age and level of health. You should confirm with your client the type of exercise their dog is accustomed to. Younger, bigger dogs, especially those bred for hunting or running, will need more exercise than elderly, small, or sick dogs. Your appointment might include time playing with them and their toys and walking them or letting them run at a dog park. When walking the dog in public, keep your charges away from other dogs and people. If the dog is attacked or harms someone else, you will be responsible. Though many dogs are friendly, you cannot risk the chance of someone getting hurt.

Small dogs, sometimes referred to as "toys" or "lap dogs," are the easiest to handle. To carry a puppy or small dog, place one hand under the dog's chest, with either your forearm or other hand supporting the hind legs and rump. Never attempt to lift or grab your puppy or small dog by the forelegs, tail, or back of the neck. If a dog is running away, do not grab it by the tail; you could snap its spine. If you do have to lift a large dog, lift from the underside, supporting his chest with one arm and his rear end with the other.

When a puppy is being house-trained or exhibits destructive behaviors, the owner may keep it in a crate. Make sure the crate has sufficient room for the dog to move around. If the dog is territorial, do not put your hands inside the cage. Instead, entice the dog out with a treat or the promise of a walk. Always check the crate for cleanliness and clean any messes right away.

Dogs are social animals and will acutely miss their owners. A bored or stressed dog might chew on items, knock over objects, or get into trash containers. If you see this behavior, try to spend a few extra minutes petting, brushing, or playing with the animal. If there are several dogs in the home, make sure they are not showing each signs of aggression due to stress.

Signs of an Aggressive Dog

A dog's motivation to bite might have several causes. There are tree types of dog aggression: fear, territorial, and dominance. The following tips will help you understand the motivators for these types of aggression and provide help to neutralize the situation.

1. **Fear Aggression:** Dogs that bite out of fear aggression will do so if they encounter an unfamiliar person or a person who incites fear through behavior such as an abrupt movement. A fearful dog will show a lowered body posture and tail position with ears pointing backwards and lips pulled back in a fearful grin. These animals might give single bites or snaps and then act in withdrawal and submissiveness. If you see a dog with this body language and behavior, do not hug, stare at, punish, or make any overt action toward it. Speak in a calm manner, and let the dog come to you. If the dog is not exhibiting the typical postures of fear, reward the dog with a treat. This will help reduce his or her fear on subsequent visits.

2. **Dominance Aggression:** A dominant dog can show this type of aggression if the dog is challenged over an object or area. The body language of dominant aggressive dogs will include eyes staring, head up, tail up, stiff gait, growling, and bared teeth. These dogs resent being reached out to, patted on the head, pushed off favored sleeping sites, or having their food approached. Be careful if you see this type of behavior; dogs who snap due to dominance aggression can give multiple, severe bites. To

reduce the risk of biting in this type of behavior, avoid standing over or staring at the dog, petting the dog for prolonged periods (especially on the head or back), and verbal or physical reprimands. Avoid taking an item from the dog or being close to food or food-related toys. Watch for these signs on your first interview with a client, and take them seriously. You cannot take care of your other responsibilities if you are sidelined by a serious bite.

3. **Territorial Aggression:** Some dogs feel an overwhelming sense of protection for their home. Dogs have different boundaries for the area they consider their personal territory. Some dogs react aggressively if a person approaches their crate or bed. Others show aggression toward intruders in the house, the garden, or the area that surrounds the owner's home. A dog showing territorial aggression will show either a lowered body or tail posture with ears laid back or may display dominance aggression traits such as staring, head and tail up, and a stiff gait. Ask the client at the first interview if the dog is territorial about any areas, and be sure to avoid these areas. A dog that is territorially aggressive to intruders in the home may not be a pet that can be cared for by a pet sitter. Bites may be a single quick bite or snap, and these dogs tend to withdraw afterward.

Dogs may also become aggressive around strange dogs, or may attack when in severe distress or pain. As part of your pet sitting kit, you may want to carry several sizes of muzzles to protect yourself or others in an emergency. If you do not have a muzzle handy, you can make one from a long piece of cloth such as a tie or a long bandana. Fold or twist the fabric into a lasso and loop it over the dog's muzzle, crossing it under its neck and tying it behind the ears.

If you are walking a dog and another dog attacks him, enlist the help of another human to break apart the fight. Each person should grab the hind legs of one of the dogs and pull them apart. The dogs may swing around to attack the person holding its legs. Make sure you keep swinging around to keep the front end away from you. The fight should dissipate soon. You may also consider carrying pepper spray or vinegar water to ward off aggressive dogs. A shot of vinegar water in the eyes will distract the other dog long enough for you to get away with your dog.

Health

Dogs may enjoy a good brushing, and your client may have you write a grooming service into the contract. Check for fleas and ticks daily during warm weather. If you find a tick, do not attempt to yank it out of the skin, which will leave the head embedded in the animal. Instead, smother it with cooking oil or petroleum jelly until the tick is unable to breathe, and it will back out of the skin in 10 to 15 minutes.

During your initial interview, you should make sure the dog has had all vaccinations and a health checkup at the veterinarian. This safeguards the pets that you will visit after this one. Dogs should have a yearly five-in-one vaccine that prevents distemper, parvovirus, parainfluenza, hepatitis, and leptospirosis. All dogs should also have a yearly rabies vaccination.

A dog's most common injury is a cut to the pads of its paws. A cut should be washed and bandaged, but a puncture may require a trip to the veterinarian.

A sick dog might be apathetic, have discharge from the eyes or nose, or show signs of pain. Most injuries, illnesses, and poisonings cause a change in one or more of three canine vital signs. Knowing a dog's normal body temperature, resting heart rate, and resting respiratory rate can help you determine if something is wrong with its health.

1. **Temperature.** The normal range for a dog's temperature is 99° Fahrenheit to 102.5° Fahrenheit. The temperature can be checked with a rectal

thermometer, either the mercury or digital kind. If you use a mercury thermometer, shake it until the reading drops below 99° Fahrenheit. Lubricate the bulb with K-Y® Jelly or petroleum jelly. Straddle the dog, facing his rump. Hold your legs firmly around his abdomen to keep him secure while you grasp his tail and insert the thermometer one inch into the rectum. Continue holding his tail and the thermometer for 60 seconds. Remove the thermometer and read the temperature.

2. **Resting Heart Rate.** Depending on the breed, the resting heart rate may vary widely.

- **Large-breed dogs** (Newfoundlands, Rottweilers, Golden Retrievers, and similar size breeds over 50 pounds) have a normal rate of 70 to 120 beats per minute.

- **Medium dogs** (Border Collies, Cocker Spaniels, and other breeds weighing 25 to 50 pounds) have a normal rate of 80 to 120 beats per minute.

- **Small dogs** (Miniature Poodles, Boston Terriers, Miniature Schnauzers and other breeds between 10 and 25 pounds) have a normal rate of 90 to 140 beats per minute.

- **Toy dogs** (Chihuahuas, Maltese and Yorkshire Terriers, and others under ten pounds) have a normal rate of 100 to 160 beats per minute.

To take the heart rate, place a clock or watch with a second hand on a chair or table near you. Straddle the dog, with his head facing away from you. Put both hands on his ribs, below his shoulders. Move your hands until you can feel his heartbeat. Count the number of beats in 15 seconds, and multiply by four; or count for 30 seconds and multiply by two.

3. **Resting Respiratory Rate.** A dog normally takes between 15 and 30 breaths per minute. Using a clock or watch with a second hand, count the number of breaths for one minute. However, if a dog is panting due to heat, shortness of breath, excitement, or pain, you will notice a different rate. Dogs with heavy coats will pant more in hot weather, and dogs with flat faces such as Pugs and Bulldogs will pant more than other breeds.

Each of these vital signs may be an important clue if you have arrived to find a sick animal and you need to make a call to the veterinarian to determine what to do next.

Case Study: Christi Marks

Christi Marks

All Tails Pet Care

Green Bay, Wisconsin

You have to be pretty fearless of animals to be successful as a pet sitter. If someone calls for you to pet sit for their two pit bulls (using them only because of the bad reputation they have been given) you cannot take on that job unless you are comfortable with the pet you are sitting for.

Be good to the animals; treat them as you would treat your own. They respond to kindness. You are entering their territory. Be aware of that. It might take a second for them to sniff your hand before they are relaxed.

Always be aware when taking dogs for walks that some dogs may be as nice as can be to you but around other dogs they are unsure and not comfortable. Be aware of your surroundings at all times and know the pets personality and temperament as best you can.

Cats

Cats were domesticated sometime between 4,000 and 8,000 years ago in Africa and the Middle East. Small wild cats started hanging out where humans stored their grain. When humans saw cats up close and personal, they began to admire felines for their beauty and grace.

There are many breeds of cats, from the hairless Sphynx and the fluffy Persian to the Manx, who has no tail. As with dogs, some varieties of cats come with special problems. Long-haired breeds can have matted hair while hairless cats to be sensitive to cold. Typical pet cats are simple mixed breeds of domestic short- or long-haired cats.

Feeding

An adult cat should be fed one large meal or two to three smaller meals each day. Kittens from six to 12 weeks old must eat four times each day. Kittens from three to six months need to be fed three times a day. A cat is one of many animals that have difficulty adjusting to changes in diet. If the cat runs out of food while you are caring for it, be sure to buy exactly the same food.

If the owner asks you to feed the cat canned food, you should throw away any leftovers in 30 to 60 minutes. The owner may ask you to serve a portion of a can each day and leave the remainder securely wrapped in the refrigerator. Other owners leave dry food available at all times, since cats tend to nibble their food throughout the day and most cats do not tend to gorge themselves uncontrollably. Monitor the food the cat is eating, as this can be one of the first signs of a problem. Cats must have fresh, clean water at all times, and pet sitters should wash and refill food and water bowls daily.

Although cat owners used to give their pets a saucer of milk, cats do not easily digest cow's milk, which can cause diarrhea or vomiting. Many cats love treats in moderation. Some pet owners train their cats to come at the sound of a treat bag being shaken, which can benefit you if the pet is hiding during your appointment. Cats may like fresh fruits and vegetables such as broccoli, corn, or cantaloupe, and your client may ask you to include these in their food bowl. Many cats also like to nibble on houseplants in normal times, but others eat leaves only when in distress. You may want to ask the owner about their kitty's habits.

Some cats enjoy catnip as a special treat and will love the chance to roll around in a little sprinkled on the ground or wrapped in a toy. However, some cats can be over-stimulated by it and can get aggressive with other pets after exposure. Be cautious if the owner provides this treat, and double check that the cats are acting normally before you leave.

If a kitten is refusing food or is not eating enough, try soaking the kitten food in warm water. If that does not work, kittens can be fed human baby food. Use turkey or chicken baby food made for children six months and older. Gradually mix with her regular food and wean her from the baby food as soon as possible.

Most cats stay relatively clean and rarely need a bath, but they need periodic brushing. Long-haired breeds, such as Persians or Maine Coon cats, should be brushed every few days to ensure snarls and mats do not develop. Cats have less tolerance for grooming than dogs, but some cats learn to love the attention. Ask your client what grooming requirements are necessary for their pet, and make sure they leave the grooming tools in an easily-found place.

Cats are extremely sensitive and clean animals. If they have an aversion to a dirty litter box they will use a corner of the carpet or a closet. Regularly scoop waste and change litter frequently to prevent the cat from making a mess somewhere else. Check with the client to verify whether it is safe to flush litter waste down the toilet.

Cats spend a good portion of each day sleeping and are often more active at night. If the cat seems unusually lethargic or disoriented, this may signal a problem. A bored or stressed cat will chew on items, knock over objects, and get into trash containers.

To pick up a cat, place one hand behind the front legs and another under the hindquarters. Lift gently, giving pressure to both areas. Never pick up a cat by the scruff of the neck or by the front legs, and never pull or grab a cat by the tail — you can break its back. If you need to restrain a cat, wrap it in a towel so that all four legs are secured.

Most cats will appreciate some petting and play time when you arrive for your appointment. In your initial interview, ask the client about the cat's favorite toys and ways of playing, and try to imitate that. Make sure you talk to the cat, too, even if you are just giving a running commentary on your day. The cat will feel less lonely.

If the cat has its own sleeping area, shake out the bedding and wash it if the client has asked you to do so. Many cats sleep just about anywhere. You should ascertain whether any areas are off-limits. If the cat is allowed outside, check it for fleas and ticks when it comes inside. Never leave the home until the cat is safely back inside. If the cat is not allowed outside, you may need to be extra vigilant every time you open a door or window. Cats are master escape artists that take advantage of any opportunity.

Like any other animal, cats have clear signals to communicate with humans. It is important to recognize the signals to maintain a good relationship with your charge and to avoid injury. Cats that are enjoying your petting will wind their bodies around your legs, rub their faces against your hand, or even roll over and let you pet their stomach for a short time. This is a sign of trust. An alert cat will have ears pointed forward and head up; when playing, their hindquarters might rise and they might wiggle their tails. An irritated cat will show displeasure by laying ears partially back and flipping its tail around. If you pet a cat showing these signals, you might be nipped and scratched. An angry, aggressive cat will hunch its body together, raise its fur, lay its ears completely back, and hiss or growl. Do not approach a cat that is showing these signals, and keep an eye on it as you move away.

Health

Cats are often more stoic and less active than dogs, and signs of illness may be harder to detect. Sick cats will often display lethargy or inactivity, lack of appetite, vomiting or diarrhea. Because cats are self-grooming, they often suffer from hair balls. Some cats eject the hair ball after a series of coughs. Any disgorged matter that contains hair balls may be a matter of no concern, but cats who vomit yellow or green substances warrant a call to the veterinarian.

Serious problems may be detected by checking the animal's vital signs. If you need to check in with a veterinarian about a cat that seems ill, he or she will find it helpful to know these indications of health.

1. **Temperature.** The normal range for a cat's temperature is 100° Fahrenheit to 102.5° Fahrenheit. The temperature can be checked with a rectal thermometer, either the mercury or digital kind. If you use a mercury thermometer, shake it until the reading drops below 99° Fahrenheit. Lubricate the bulb with K-Y® Jelly or petroleum jelly. Wrap the cat in a towel with only its head and rear showing; hold the cat firmly under one arm. Grasp his tail and insert the thermometer one inch into the rectum. Continue holding his tail and the thermometer for 60 seconds. Remove the thermometer and read the temperature.

2. **Resting Heart Rate.** The normal value in a cat's heart rate ranges from 120 to 200 depending on how excited he is. A cat's heart rate can be checked either by feeling his heart beat or counting the beats from his femoral artery. Place your fingertips on the inside of your cat's upper

leg close to the body to feel the pulse of the femoral artery. To check the heart beating through the chest wall, hold the chest between your thumb and fingers at the point where the elbow would touch it if it were flexed. To measure the pulse or heart rate, place a clock or watch with a second hand on a chair or table near you. Count the number of pulses of the femoral artery or the heartbeats you feel in 15 seconds and multiply that number by four or count for 30 seconds and multiply by two.

3. **Resting Respiratory Rate.** A cat's respiratory rate has a wide range. A sleeping cat may take 30 breaths per minute. A cat that is agitated or in pain may take 100 breaths per minute. The respiratory rate is measured by counting the number of times the cat's chest moves in and out in 15 seconds and multiplying that number by four. A cat that is panicking or in pain may begin to pant.

It is also useful to determine how the cat is breathing. Heavy or labored breathing is a sign of respiratory or other problems. Cats with respiratory distress will often inhale for a much longer time than they exhale. Cats with breathing difficulties may exhale with greater effort and use their abdominal muscles to press the air from their lungs.

Birds

Cockatiels, parrots, parakeets, and finches are some of the most popular birds for pet owners. Bird lovers enjoy their pets because of their beautiful songs, funny antics, and graceful behavior. Birds require a cage large enough to accommodate their wingspan, and the cage should offer a perch or two. Birds can be sensitive to cold or drafts; carefully watch the temperature while the client is gone. Owners may provide a cloth to cover the bird either to reduce distractions so the bird can sleep or to cut down on drafts. Ask the owner about his or her practice when it comes to covering the cage.

Feeding

Different breeds of birds have different nutritional requirements. Breed-specific bird feed mixes are a mixture of seeds, formulated foods, supplements, and additional vitamins. Bird mixes are regarded as suitable, especially when provided with additional supplements. Formulated diets, pelletized or extruded, contain all the necessary minerals and vitamins. Additional vitamins are not required. However, formulated diets do not contain the phytonutrients found in vegetables, fruits, grains, and seeds. Phytonutrients are believed to boost the immune system, help a body heal itself, and prevent some diseases. Many birds also become bored with a formulated diet due to the lack of variety. Offering supplements can help provide the phytonutrients and help offset boredom.

Seed-only diets offer more variety, but require additional vitamin and calcium supplements. In the wild, birds ,may eat seed as a major portion of their diet. Many birds need not only nutrition, but also variety. To provide a balanced diet, minerals, amino acids, vitamins and trace elements can be added as a supplement to seed or water.

Supplements include soaked and sprouted seeds, fruits, vegetables, and non-toxic green plants. All types of fruits such as apples, pears, plums, cherries, grapes, oranges, bananas, mangos, papayas, and berries make good supplements. Vegetables such as carrots, cucumbers, zucchini, and others also are good supplements. Dandelions and chickweed work as well. Do not feed avocado, as it may be toxic to birds. Some owners occasionally feed their birds protein such as cottage cheese, hard boiled eggs, or canned dog food.

Cuttlebone and calcium blocks will also provide necessary minerals for maintaining a bird's health. These blocks are often clipped to the side of the cage.

Some seed-eating birds need grit. This applies especially to birds like pigeons and doves that eat their seed whole without shelling it first. These birds will store the grit in their crops to grind the seed. Ask your client about specific dietary needs and the order in which they offer the bird food and nutrients.

Birds need a steady supply of water. Many owners clip a tube of water to the side of the cage; this water should be changed daily. Bird owners may also leave a bowl of water inside the cage for the bird to use in bathing. Some birds enjoy a light daily misting to hydrate their skin.

After feeding and watering the bird, clean the cage and the food bowls. Bird owners line the cage with newspaper, wood chips, or other materials. Make sure the bird is not chewing on the bedding. Replace these materials according to the owner's instructions, and make sure the cage is clean.

You may be asked to care for birds nesting eggs or have hatchlings. If so, take extra care to not disturb the nest or agitate the birds while cleaning and feeding. Do not try to clean the nest unless you find a dead bird among the hatchlings; remove it gently while trying not to disturb the others. Make sure you understand any other special care requirements for the nesting brood before the owner leaves.

Birds enjoy free time outside a cage; ask your client if the bird likes to be uncaged. Be sure it is safe to let the bird out of the cage. Do not leave windows and doors open. Look for hazards, such as water-filled vessels, a hot stove, an open window, or a running ceiling fan. Do not let your bird eat any toxic plants such as oleanders, azaleas, juniper, daffodils, philodendron, lily-of-the-valley, or dumb cane.

If the bird is squawking incessantly, fluttering around the cage, or pecking the other birds, it may need some help to calm down. Speak in a low, calm tone to the bird. Try turning on soothing music and turning up the heat just a bit so that it feels warmer and more calm. If the bird is puffing up its chest and pecking at your hand while you care for it, the pet may be trying to display dominance. Height is a dominance feature for birds. You could try moving the cage so that your face is above the bird.

Health

Signs of good health in a bird include bright eyes, shiny feathers, good appetite, and lots of energy. Healthy birds eat often and are active. If a bird is upset it will ruffle its feathers, puff itself up to seem larger, thrust its head forward, and snap at its enemy. While many birds enjoy landing on a human's hand, shoulder, or head, watch out for those who scratch or have a bad habit of nipping. Find out about the bird's personality before sitting for it the first time.

The most common injuries to birds are broken wings or toenails. Birds can bleed to death quickly, and you will need to act immediately. If a bird is hurt, gently restrain the bird in a towel or blanket to prevent it from thrashing around and hurting itself further. When the injury is a bleeding toenail, pack it with cornstarch or flour and apply pressure. Hold the pressure for at least five minutes. After the bleeding has stopped, you can release the bird; if it is still bleeding, maintain the pressure until the blood clots.

If a bird has broken a blood feather and has been thrashing around in its cage, it may have splashed blood around. Calmly catch the bird in a towel or blanket and check carefully to see what is going on. If the feather shaft is broken, remove it with a pair of pliers, and pack the injury with flour or cornstarch and apply gentle pressure, being careful not to squeeze the bird too tightly.

When birds are sick or injured, they may try to hide their illness as a survival instinct. However, signs of illness include closed or swollen eyes, diarrhea, fecal stains on the feathers surrounding the vent (anus), noisy or labored breathing with wheezing or clicking sounds, or perching in one place with feathers fluffed up for a long time during the day.

Fish

Many fish owners love aquariums because watching the fish swim around is a soothing experience. Fish can be easy to care for, but some have special needs. Aquarium owners may have a special gadget that disperses food and nutrients into the water, and they might not even need a sitter. Those that have elaborate or sensitive fish will need a pet sitter who can provide special attention.

There are three basic types of aquariums:.

1. **Saltwater aquariums** contain fish and other animals from ocean environments.

2. **Freshwater aquariums** contain fish and plants from lakes, streams, and other freshwater sources.

3. **Reef aquariums**, which may not contain any fish at all, will house other saltwater animals and plants such as coral, sea anemones, and mollusks.

If you are not familiar with any of these, ask the client to provide you with detailed instructions.

Your sitting job will likely consist of checking the conditions of the tank and feeding the fish. There are a variety of fish foods depending on the breed. You may have to provide fresh, frozen, or dried foods to these pets. One of the most common mistakes in caring for fish is feeding them too much. As a basic rule, a fish's eye is about the same size as its stomach. The fish may need less food than you think. Fish will eat only until they are full, and the rest of the food falls to the bottom of the tank.

Tanks may be equipped with a thermometer and a heater. You should check these every day to be sure the temperature remains within the client's stated normal range. Aquariums also have a water filter that bubbles mixing oxygen into the water. During each visit, you should verify that these are working properly and rinse out the filter if it is blocked. If the water becomes cloudy or the walls become heavy with green or brown algae, you must clean the tank. Owners may have a vacuum-like tool to siphon waste from the floor of the tank and algae from the walls. Be sure you know how to use these tools, and be careful not to suck up a fish along with the dirt.

You should also count the fish at each visit. Fish can be aggressive and have been known to eat each other as well as their own babies. If a fish spawns while you are caring for the aquarium, you may want to separate the small fry into another container for their own safety. Some especially aggressive fish attack smaller fish; keep careful watch over breeds such as Angelfish and Bettas.

Fish are sensitive to temperature changes, chemicals, and loud noises. For these reasons, an aquarium should never be located near a heating duct or a sunny window. If you are responsible for opening and closing blinds, make sure that opening the blinds will not expose the fish tank to too much sunlight. Whenever new water is added to the tank, you must add certain chemicals to condition the water. Try not to put your hands in the water as you will add unhealthy contaminants to the water. Some fish, such as the piranha or eel, might nip your fingers, and some anemones are poisonous. Do not tap on the glass, even if you are worried about a fish's lack of movement. The noise will be magnified in the water, and will be unbearably loud to the fish.

Examine any live plants in the tank and remove rotting or diseased-looking plants. If there are snails on the plants, be sure to pick them off and put them back into the tank.

Healthy fish swim easily, though they may hover in one area or hide in a plant or corner. Many fish will rush to the surface when you feed them. A sick fish may swim around in circles or float upside down. A dead fish will float belly-up at the top or bottom of the tank unless another fish has eaten it. Some fish are short-lived or are so sensitive to environment that they die easily. If you find a dead fish, scoop it out with a net and save it in a plastic bag for the owner unless you have other instructions. You may want to store it in their freezer until the owner returns home.

Other signs of sickness include a film or veil of material around the fish, especially around the eyes, fins, and gills. Tropical fish are also susceptible to fin rot, where the presenting condition is ragged-looking fins, and white spot disease, where white patches of bacteria will grow on the scales. Your resources for fish problems might include specialty fish stores that can offer medicine and advice or a veterinarian with experience in treating fish. Since transporting a fish is an extremely stressful experience for the animal, call for help rather than taking the fish to the specialist.

Amphibians

There is a bewildering variety of frogs, including land, tree, and water frogs. Some frogs rarely leave the water, and some must have dry land to live on. If you are sitting for a client that has pet frogs, follow their instructions exactly. Frogs can be delicate and sensitive to contaminants in the environment.

Some frogs and toads secrete toxins. It is wise to handle them as little as possible. If you must pick up a toad, wash your hands in clean water first and leave them wet. Never touch your eyes, mouth or face when you are handling an amphibian, and thoroughly wash your hands afterward.

Frogs and toads may live in an aquarium with a tight-fitting lid with a fluorescent light and ventilation space in the rear. These aquariums must be kept away from windows and heating/cooling vents. The floor may be covered with aquarium gravel and smooth rocks that form dry islands, and the aquarium may have live plants. The owner may ask you to wash down the walls and rocks with a spray bottle of de-chlorinated water to remove toxins secreted by the toads.

At each pet sitting visit, check the thermometer to be sure the water temperature is between 65 and 75 degrees F. The amphibians can be hard to see in the foliage or underwater, but make sure you count all the pets each time you visit. Some frogs may be hard to see. Check to be sure they are all in place.

The type of food provided to these pets will depend on the breed, but most frogs eat insects and larva, and you will be handling insects if you take on a frog-sitting job. The client may feed the amphibians a specialized diet or may provide waxworms and crickets. Each amphibian should get two small waxworms or two small crickets per week. The larger frog breeds can eat whole live crickets. Be sure you understand your feeding responsibilities before you take the job. If you are squeamish about feeding live creatures to a pet, this may not be the client for you.

Amphibians are healthy. They change color from bright green to dark olive green when they are about to shed. Check for dull eyes, heavy breathing, or trouble swimming, as these are signs of sickness. A specialty pet store or a veterinarian with experience in treating amphibians can help if you suspect that one of the pets is ill.

Reptiles

Reptile lovers are fans of their pets because they are quiet and have virtually no odor. There are a huge variety of reptiles from the tiny anole to the Komodo Dragon. Common reptile pets include snakes, lizards, turtles, and salamanders. Since most reptiles do not need much room, they can be an ideal pet for small apartments or a child's room. Reptiles are easy to take care of with a minimum amount of cleaning. They can even survive missing a feeding. In nature, reptiles do not eat every day, and they have to be more active in collecting their food than they do in captivity.

Reptiles cannot regulate their own body temperatures, and a pet reptile relies on its owner to provide optimal conditions for it to live. Owners may provide a tank or cage fitted for the particular breed. Snakes, lizards, and tortoises may have cages lined with newspaper, AstroTurf®, or paper towels. Owners often use shredded paper, old T-shirts, or towels for burrowing animals; other creatures must have special rock or sand material called substrate for the bottom of their homes. These linings must be cleaned or replaced regularly. While some lizards need a desert-like habitat, other creatures need a moist, mossy home. Make sure you know how often the cage or tank should be cleaned and where you can find new bedding supplies. Turtles need both wet and easily-accessed dry areas. Keep water clean and at 70° to 75° Fahrenheit.

Because most reptiles need an environment warmer than room temperature, most owners install a heat lamp or warming rock to keep the temperature in the 80's during the day, and in the 70's at night. Ask the owner about the temperature settings, and be sure to check this during each visit. Snakes, and some lizards, like hiding places. Check these areas after you arrive for your appointment if the reptile is not immediately visible. When you are caring for reptiles, pay attention to the following:

1. All food and water dishes should be cleaned daily.

2. Do not leave fresh food out for more than 12 hours.

3. Clean cages that have paper bedding every other day, and those with AstroTurf® one to two times each week.

4. Wash your hands after caring for reptiles, especially when handling turtles, to decrease the risk of salmonella infection.

Reptiles eat a variety of foods, depending on the breed. Some reptiles are carnivores, some eat only insects, some are vegetarians, and some eat anything. Follow your client's instructions exactly; reptiles can overeat or become congested with the wrong types of food. If a client asks you to care for a reptile, know that you will need to be able to feed a live baby mouse or a cricket to the pet before you take the job.

1. **Snakes:** Any frozen food must be fully thawed before feeding. Most larger snakes will eat rodents, but Ring Snakes will eat amphibians and earthworms, while Garter and Water snakes will eat goldfish. Prey should be freshly killed or thawed. Juveniles are fed once daily, and adults are fed once or twice weekly.

2. **Lizards:** Vegetarians are often fed washed, chopped, and mixed leafy greens, carrots, squash, sweet potatoes, thawed frozen mixed vegetables, alfalfa, radish, clover, bean sprouts, soaked alfalfa pellets, mushrooms, bell peppers, green beans, and okra. They might also eat small amounts of apples, pears, grapes, plums, oranges, nectarines, figs, seedless melon, bananas, and grape fruit. Clean up any uneaten food daily.Insectivores are fed crickets, mealworms, earthworms, grasshoppers, and other insects available at pet food stores.

3. **Turtles:** These reptiles might eat whole animals such as earthworms, slugs, crickets, mealworms, thawed frozen or fresh goldfish,

guppies, trout, bait fish, and smelt. Some turtles are omnivorous and might eat some of the same plant materials as lizards. Owners may feed hatchlings once a day, and adults one to three times a week.

All reptiles need fresh water daily. You might provide the water through misting, spraying, or a water dish. A deep dish holds the risk of drowning the reptile. Be cautious. Water contaminated with feces or urine should be changed immediately. For insectivores, water bowls should be partially filled with rocks that rise above the water line so no insects drown and foul the water.

Some lizards are escape artists. Do not give them any opportunities. Snakes in particular can squeeze through small holes. If a reptile is lost, the most likely place to find them is in a dark place such as underneath couch cushions or in a heating duct. You can try to entice them out with food. For your own safety, follow the handling advice the client gives you. Many lizards and snakes are poisonous, and most reptiles have claws that can inflict harm. Some turtles can snap off a finger with their beaks. If you are sitting for a snake that squeezes its prey to death, such as a python or a boa constrictor, do not allow it to wrap itself around any part of your body, regardless of the snake's age or size. The best way to handle a snake is to grip it right behind the head and hold the tail with your other hand. Many snake owners will also have a handling pole or snake hook that they use to restrain the pet. Ask them to demonstrate its use on your interview visit.

If a reptile is sick, you may see the pet acting lethargic or losing weight. However, some reptiles are naturally lethargic. It is important to find out the pet's personality so that any changes are obvious. Normally sedate lizards that act agitated might have a problem. It is normal for lizards to shed skin periodically; some lizards can also shed part of their tail as an escape measure. Snakes shed their skin in one piece, while lizards shed in patches. If you see any sneezing, wheezing, or foamy discharges from the mouth or nose, call a veterinarian. Other signs of sickness include the inability to use limbs, walk or move, swollen eyes, lumps on the body, a swollen jaw, bubbles or red areas at the mouth, red areas, and, in females, a swollen abdomen, restless digging, and straining. Chameleons are prone to jaw infections caused by lodged insect parts. All of these conditions require veterinary care.

Rodents

Hamsters, gerbils, rats, guinea pigs, and mice are popular rodent pets. These animals are particularly attractive because they do not take up much room and can be playful. Rodents are more active at night and can be noisy.

Pet rodents are kept in cages or aquarium tanks. Absorbent materials, such as white wood shavings or shredded newspapers, are used to line the cage bottom. Gerbils and hamsters like to dig and burrow; adding a layer of peat moss allows them to exercise this behavior. The cage must be cleaned at least once each week, and new shavings should be placed on the floor. Inside the cage, rodents may have a cardboard or wooden nesting area, toys such as plastic tubes and small boxes, some shredded tissue for nest building, and an exercise wheel for smaller rodents. Always check the cage to make sure it is secure, because rodents, especially hamsters and rats, are escape artists.

Rodents must have fresh food and clean water daily, and their dishes should be cleaned regularly. Many owners clip a water bottle to the side of the cage that dispenses water as the animal needs it. The bottle should be low enough that even the smallest animal can reach it. Your client will likely have commercial pelletized foods for their particular species of rodent. The pelletized food should be available for the rodent at all times. Hamsters, gerbils, mice and rats are omnivores. They enjoy being offered fresh fruit, seeds, nuts, and vegetables to supplement the commercial pelletized food. During each visit, be sure to remove any uneaten fresh food so that it will not spoil. Hamsters and gerbils will tend to hoard food. Do not be surprised to find hidden caches of food when you clean the cage. Be sure to remove their food stash before it spoils.

Rodents like being handled gently, petted, and played with, but they will bite if they are handled quickly or roughly. To pet a rodent, slowly pick it up by cradling or cupping your hands, and placing the animal on a flat surface with a bit of food. Gently stroke their back. If you take the rodent outside of its cage, keep a sharp eye on it. They are quick little creatures and can run away quickly requiring you to run and catch them.

Lumps, bumps, and broken legs are rodents' most common medical problems. Broken bones are often sustained from falls; it is best to handle the animal while sitting down. Stress can be a big problem for rodents, especially if there are many animals in the nest, if there are environmental changes or poor diet, or if the cage mates do not get along. Sometimes a female under stress will eat her litter of babies.

Since many rodents sleep during the day and are active at night, you may have difficulty assessing their health. Always make sure they have eaten and that they have drunk sufficient water to maintain their health. Signs of illness include erratic behavior such as walking in circles, dull fur coats, discharge from the eyes or nose, or self-mutilation. If the rodents under your care show problems such as diarrhea, hair loss, excessive water drinking, or not eating, call a veterinarian. Separate the sick rodent from the other rodents until you are sure the illness is not contagious.

Ferrets

Ferret owners love their pets because of their curiosity, energy, playfulness, and intelligence. Ferrets are quite active and require training and care; be prepared for your ferret to command your daily attention. Ferrets are not rodents; they are actually members of the weasel family that also includes minks. Some states and cities prohibit the ownership of ferrets.

Ferrets live in cages that allow them to climb with a little den area where they can retreat. Ferrets can be sensitive to heat, and their cages should not be placed in direct sunlight. The owner will likely put down shredded material or AstroTurf® in the cage. This material must be cleaned and changed often. Some owners have trained their animals to use a small litter box. If this is the case, make sure you keep this area clean. Ferrets can be messy animals, and much of your pet sitting appointment will be spent cleaning up after them.

One notable characteristic of the ferret is the scent glands they use to mark their territory. This leaves a strong, musky odor around the ferret and its cage unless the owner has had the scent glands removed. Some people find the odor unpleasant. The owner may ask you to give the ferret a bath using pet or baby shampoo. The ferret may enjoy this grooming time.

As with all pets, ferrets need plenty of clean water and a fresh supply of food each day. Your client should have food designed specifically for ferrets; dog or cat food is not healthy for them. Wash their dishes after each use.

Ferrets are social creatures that enjoy visiting with people; if your client allows the ferret outside the cage, let them roam in a secure area. Make time to play with the animal. If it gets bored, it may become destructive and chew up items in its cage. Although they have a strong sense of smell and acute hearing, ferrets have limited vision; do not make any sudden movements. Speak in a gentle voice before approaching them. Because ferrets have fragile skeletons, be sure to handle them carefully. Never pick up a ferret by the tail. Instead, let the ferret come to you and lift him from behind using two hands. Use one hand to support his chest and one to cradle his hips. You can also grasp the scruff of a ferret's neck and support his bottom with your hands.

Because ferrets like to nip, keep your fingers away from its mouth. Be careful with its claws, too. These are energetic animals that may inadvertently scratch you while they are wiggling around. Some ferrets can be aggressive, especially with strangers, and you will need to proceed with caution until you are familiar with his or her personality. In the wild, ferrets are hunting animals that might pose problems to cats or small pets. Be careful.

Ferrets play with bursts of energy and then sleep deeply. If you see the ferret sleeping all the time, this is normal.

Ferrets have a habit of swallowing indigestible articles, such as rubber bands or pieces of vinyl toys, causing intestinal blockage. Persistent vomiting, loss of appetite, lethargy, and dehydration are indications of blockage. If you notice these signs, you should take the ferret to the veterinarian immediately. Other problem signs warranting veterinary attention are blood in the urine, severe hair loss, breathing difficulty, inability to urinate, dramatic weight loss, lethargy and weakness, loss of color in gums, and scratching or chewing of paws.

Rabbits

Rabbits are popular companion animals and backyard pets. As pets, rabbits are small, relatively easy to care for, and quiet. Some varieties are large and have specific grooming requirements. Some owners have litter box-trained these pets. Rabbits are timid animals that respond best to calm motions and soothing noises.

Owners may feed rabbits a high quality, high fiber pelletized food. Loose hay, such as mixed grass hay, timothy hay or high-quality grass clipping, may also offered. Alfalfa hay can be offered during the growth stage but should then be discontinued due to its high protein content. Owners may supplement a rabbit's diet with leafy greens such as Kale or mustard greens, fresh vegetables such as carrots or broccoli, and a small amount of fruit such as strawberries or apples. A proper diet is essential because nutritional problems are common in pet rabbits.

Rabbits produce two types of fecal pellets: Mucus pellets and dry (hard) pellets. The mucus pellet is a night feces, produced in the early morning hours, and immediately ingested by the rabbit. It is a source of B vitamins, amino acids, and fatty acids. The dry pellets are not normally ingested.

Rabbits may also suffer from hair balls. High-fiber diets, minimal stress and boredom, and frequent brushing can prevent hair balls. Hair balls can cause rabbits to stop eating. Feeding fresh pineapple juice has reportedly aided in the breakdown and passage of hair balls. Long-haired rabbits will require brushing, and long- or flop-ear breeds will need to have their ears cleaned and checked.

Owners keep rabbits in well-ventilated and easy-to-clean cages. The cages are often lined with grass hay, wood chips, or pelletized cellulose. This material should be changed every few days. Put the rabbit in a safe room or alternate cage as you sweep out the cage and scrub the floor with warm, soapy water The cage should be situated where the rabbit will not be able to chew on power cords, books, or other objects.

A rabbit's ears are highly vascular, fragile, and sensitive and should not be used for restraint. The rabbit skeleton is also fragile, making the lumbar spine susceptible to fracture. It is important to hold rabbits properly and securely to avoid struggling that can lead to broken backs. Rabbits can be carried by grasping the loose skin over the shoulders with one hand, tucking the rabbit's head under one arm, and placing the other arm under the rump to support the weight. For restraint, a towel works well.

A rabbit rarely makes any noise but will squeal if in extreme distress. Rabbits do not enjoy being suddenly lifted up, and they become anxious when airborne. Let the rabbit hop around on its own, and pet it in the position it chooses. Rabbits often like to smell a human's hand before being petted and prefer being petted on the forehead and spine rather than on the sides and belly. If it enjoys your petting, the rabbit may click its teeth together quietly — sort of a bunny version of purring.

An upset rabbit will hop away, showing its rear legs and tail. It may turn its back to you as a sign of extreme displeasure. If you keep pursuing it, it may lunge at you, growl, and snap at you. Give the rabbit some time to cool down before approaching it again.

Ask your client if the rabbit has any special grooming requirements. Long-haired and curly-haired varieties of rabbits need frequent combing or brushing. Always brush from the back of the head down to the tail. If the owner will be gone for a long time, ask him or her to show you how to clip its nails and teeth, or require them to take care of these tasks before you sit for the animal.

Rabbits are susceptible to many health problems, with complications due to obesity being one of the most common. Make sure the rabbit in your care gets plenty of exercise time in a safe place outside its cage each day. Since rabbits tend to chew on things, make sure you keep them away from power cords or anything else they might find to nibble on. Examine the rabbit's feet, as this is a common site for infection, especially when the rabbit lives in a cage with a wire floor. Each time you visit, check for signs of illness such as labored breathing, cloudy eyes, lack of appetite, or diarrhea. Seek a veterinarian's care for these problems.

Case Study: Teresa Lewis 

Teresa Lewis

Helping Hand Animal Care

Chesapeake, Virginia

The best part of a sitting job is the love the animals show me. I once took care of a Great Dane for a friend, and he would do a little dance when I came in. I loved that dog! Another client had a sick kitty, and because I was able to care for its health, the owner was able to keep her vacation plans.

It is important to make sure that the animal and I match well. I rely on my gut feel to determine whether I can work with an animal. If you are afraid, they can sense it, and it will not work. One difficult assignment was with an Australian cattle dog named Boozer. The owner did not even need to lock up her house because the dog sounded so ferocious. I would come armed with treats. When I came up to the house after giving him treats, he was fine. Once, he even licked me!

"You can say any fool thing to a dog, and the dog will give you this look that says, `My God, you're RIGHT! I NEVER would've thought of that!'"

~Dave Barry

9

Exotic, Wild, & Farm Animals

Exotic Pets

The excitement of owning an unusual pet is one reason that extraordinary and rare animals have become popular pets. The variety of behaviors, interesting looks, and unusual needs can make exotic pets more fun than a traditional animal. There are sometimes strict laws about importing exotic animals into the United States. If someone asks you to care for a pet that you know might be on an endangered or illegal list, decline the job. It is not worth sullying your reputation.

Case Study: Miranda Murdock

CLASSIFIED CASE STUDIES™
directly from the experts

Miranda Murdock

My Pet's Buddy

Greenwood, Louisiana

Do not be afraid to accept jobs that require you to care for exotic pets just because you lack experience. I have found that educating myself on different pets, and having the client do a thorough walk through of their care provides enough information to survive a vacation pet sit.

Case Study: Miranda Murdock

I learn by communicating on Internet message boards with other sitters who have that specific expertise. I always tell the client if I do not have experience with their kind of pet. You should never mislead the customer.

Chinchillas

Chinchillas are silky-soft rodents that look like a cross between a rabbit and a large mouse. They are playful, gentle, nocturnal animals that can be quite shy. They are most active in the evening and at night and can be playful and rambunctious at these times. For this reason, you may want to schedule a pet sitting visit for these creatures at night to take advantage of their playtime. They should be kept in a quiet area during the day.

The owner will likely have established a consistent routine for handling and feeding times, since chinchillas like peace and order and may be stressed out by changes to their routine. Because they are so active and playful, chinchillas need a roomy cage for exercise. Chinchillas are more sensitive to heat than cold. Monitor the temperature of the pet's area to be sure it is not too warm. Like other rodents, a chinchilla's cage may be lined with wood shavings or newspapers which must be kept clean.

Chinchillas require roughage. The owner should provide a supply of good quality grass hay, along with pelletized food for chinchillas. Ask the client to tell you the exact amounts of each type of food. Treats should be given in moderation (one teaspoon per day in total), and can include fruits such as fresh or dried apples, grapes, or raisins. Carrots, celery, sunflower seeds, and rolled oats are also acceptable treats. The digestive system of chinchillas is fairly sensitive. Be careful with any drastic changes in diet.

In their natural habitat, chinchillas roll in dust baths to clean their fur and to groom themselves. Owners should provide an area for the animal to have a periodic dust bath, and only a special chinchilla dust should be used. Be sure to clean the cage and provide new dust every few days during your sitting visits. Since a chinchilla will shake the dust everywhere, part of your sitting tasks will be to clean up the mess in the area surrounding the cage.

Since chinchillas often take dust baths, their eyes may become irritated from the dust. Try gently wiping the eyelids with a damp cloth. Signs of illness in a chinchilla include inactivity during normal periods of activity, watery eyes, diarrhea, poor appetite, drool down the chin, wobbly or erratic pacing, or seizures. Call a veterinarian if you see these signs.

Crabs

The most common type of pet crab is the hermit crab, which can be found in any shopping mall or pet store. They are low-maintenance pets that require little setup, and can be easy for children to care for.

The appropriate temperature and humidity is critical to a crab's health. Land hermit crabs come from warm tropical climates and therefore need a warm, humid environment to survive. Most crab owners keep them in a small glass or plastic tank with a lid that helps hold in heat and humidity. Sand is typically spread on the floor, and many owners will provide rocks or pieces of clean driftwood for the creature to crawl on.

Though they are called hermits, these crabs are social creatures and are best kept in groups. Owners may provide several extra shells in varying sizes around the tanks; as a crab gets larger or molts off old skin, it will try out a new shell to see how it fits. A crab out of its shell is vulnerable and easily stressed; do not touch it unless you absolutely must.

Crabs are omnivores that eat a variety of foods. Owners often provide commercial food formulated especially for crabs supplementing this diet with fruits. Pieces of grapes, mangoes, peaches, apples, and berries are appropriate. Lettuce, spinach, broccoli, watercress, popcorn, brine shrimp, and hardboiled egg crumbs may also be included. Be sure you understand exactly what your particular charge can eat, and clean out any uneaten food on a daily basis.

Another popular crab pet is a fiddler crab, which has one large front claw and one smaller one. These crabs need to live in a saltwater environment that also includes dry land. Fiddler crabs molt just as other crabs do. The owner will likely feed them fish or shrimp pellets.

Hedgehogs

Hedgehogs are shy, nocturnal animals that can take some time to become used to being handled. They often spend much of the day sleeping and are active at night. Hedgehog owners often keep the animals in multi-level ferret or rabbit cages with an exercise wheel, toys, and an area to hide in, such as a box. Appropriate temperature is important for hedgehogs. Make sure your hedgehog's habitat is away from drafts, and keep the temperature between 68° and 80° F.

While some hedgehogs can learn to use a litter box, owners often use newspaper or wood shavings in the cage. Cedar shavings are toxic to a hedgehog's respiratory system. If you run out of litter material while caring for this type of animal, be sure to choose something non-toxic. Make sure the animal does not eat the bedding or litter material, as this can cause digestive problems. This bedding should be changed every day or every other day, but the owner is likely to have specific care instructions for you.

Hedgehogs are sensitive to foods. Some owners feed them cat food, while other owners offer special hedgehog food or low-fat foods such as steamed chicken and vegetables. If the owner has asked you to switch foods while they are gone, be sure to do it gradually by mixing a little new food with the old foods each day. Hedgehogs drink water from either a bowl or a water bottle as rodents do. Be sure the animal has plenty of fresh water each day.

Hedgehogs are prickly animals, and they tend to become nervous easily. They roll into a ball, with spines outward, when they are afraid. If you need to pick one up, use gloves and lift them from the underside of the belly where they have no spines. It is normal for young hedgehogs to lose spines as their adult spines grow in, but adults who lose spines may have a skin problem or fleas. If you see spines lying around the cage, check the skin for crustiness or signs of irritation.

To learn more about these unusual, delightful pets, you can visit the Web sites **www.chinsnquills.com**, **www.hedgies.com**, or **www.hedgehogvalley.com**.

Monkeys

Monkeys are adorable, personable, energetic pets that are often banned for sale in the United States. They require specialized care and extensive knowledge. If a client asks you to sit for a monkey, check your state and local laws before engaging in potentially illegal care.

Monkeys are one of the most intelligent animals on earth. However, they have not evolved into domesticated animals the way dogs, cats, and other animals have. Monkeys find it difficult to adapt to a home. Thus the pet owner has a challenge in caring for the animal, and as a pet sitter you will be challenged as well. Monkeys are impulsive, unpredictable and excitable; they are social animals that need interaction with you as well as food and exercise. Because of their sociability, the owner may keep more than one primate. When you first visit the monkey, move slowly and speak its name gently and softly. Make friends by offering it a piece of fruit or other treat. Let it get to know you gradually.

Some of the most popular breeds of monkeys are the small Capuchin, squirrel, and spider monkeys. Chimpanzees are larger monkeys also kept as pets. Each of these breeds are agile and clever, and they have nimble fingers. They can easily escape a cage, especially if you are not alert while caring for them. Do not underestimate the strength or the intelligence of a monkey.

The owner will keep the monkey in a tall cage with numerous play and hanging areas. Monkeys love toys, and the more toys they have to play with the less destructive they will be. The cage will likely have some natural vegetation and a heat lamp. Monkeys are tropical animals and need to have their cage temperature regulated. The cage should be swept and cleaned daily and disinfected weekly with a mild disinfectant available at a pharmacy or pet store.

Pet monkeys love to be bathed and to splash around in water. Some owners provide a little bath or water tub for their pets. The owner might ask you to give the monkey a bath using human shampoo or with a special animal shampoo. Make sure you have everything ready before bathing the animal in warm water. They will not wait around while you set everything in place. Gently brush the coat after drying the animal. Grooming is a big part of communal primate life and the monkey will likely enjoy this.

Monkeys eat a varied diet, but the owner will likely feed him a commercial primate diet. This can be supplemented with fruits, cooked vegetables such as carrots, raw vegetables, seeds, nuts, wheat bread, and boiled eggs. Some monkeys enjoy live food such as crickets, grasshoppers and mealworms. In the wild, primates feed on fruits, nuts, seeds, berries, insects, lizards, rodents, and small birds. The owner may ask you to give the animal vitamin supplements, as well. Primates commonly have a vitamin mix that can be sprinkled over their food.

Monkeys can get into anything. They have been known to disassemble their water bottles or toys. If the owner allows the monkey out of its cage, it can get into anything a child might get into. Be careful that the animal does not harm itself with electrical appliances, medicines, or household chemicals. Monkeys can also have behavioral problems, especially as they mature. They are known to bite and can attack animals or humans if depressed, enraged, or confused. Watch their behavior closely. Aggressive monkeys are also known to throw feces when upset. Larger monkeys such as chimpanzees may be much stronger than their size would indicate. Be aware when caring for these animals.

Primates are susceptible to many of the same diseases as humans, and the signs of ill health are similar. Watch for lethargy, dull eyes, discharge from the nose or mouth, and diarrhea. Make sure the animal is eating well and is active. The monkey owner might have a difficult time finding a veterinarian that treats primates. If no qualified veterinarian is available and the monkey shows signs of illness, contact the primate experts at the local zoo.

Potbelly Pigs

Pet pigs have become more popular and acceptable in the last 30 years, and they can be enjoyable pets because they are friendly, clean, and entertaining. They are easily housebroken and intelligent. The potbelly pig breed was originally imported from Asia. There are miniature versions, but this is a relative term, as these breeds will grow to over 100 pounds, compared to pig livestock that range from 300 to 1,000 pounds.

Owners of potbelly pigs keep them indoors in a space that can be confined, such as a laundry room or basement but may keep them caged outside in warm climates. Some pigs are trained to use a litter box, and others are trained to go outside. Because pigs are intelligent, they require attention and an extra measure of caution. They are on a constant search for food and can open cupboards or even the refrigerator to dig for what they are want. They can overturn trash containers and will eat from other pets' food bowls. You will have to make sure everything is secured and that nothing is left lying around for the pig to get into.

The owner will typically feed the pig either a domestic pig feed or a commercial maintenance feed. They may offer a pig occasional treats such as apples, grapes, or raisins. Be sure you understand the exact amount of food to offer, since pigs will gorge themselves. Make sure you limit treats, since the greatest health threat to pigs is obesity. Always make sure the pig always has access to plenty of clean, fresh water.

Pigs will need time outside at each visit. They have a habit of rooting around in the ground with their snouts, and will eat grass or leaves. Because they are social creatures, they will also need some attention from you during the appointment. They enjoy having their hides scratched and will listen if you talk to them. Pigs like to play with balls or other durable toys. Because they cannot sweat, they are susceptible to heat stroke and sunburn in warm weather. Many owners provide a child-sized swimming pool for the pig to wallow in. Make sure the water is clean and wipe off the animals coat and hooves before letting it back inside.

Pigs and dogs do not get along well together; it is unlikely that your client will have both pets. However, if you pass by a dog while walking the pig, know that the pig is the dog's natural prey. Keep the two animals separated.

Because obesity is a problem for these pigs, they are prone to joint problems and respiratory ailments such as pneumonia. Watch for signs including difficulty breathing, wheezing, exhaustion, loss of interest in food and activities, limping, and discharge from the nose or eyes. Pigs are becoming more familiar household pets, and it is likely that a veterinarian will have the skills to treat their problems.

Spiders and Insects

Think of a pet spider and most people imagine the scary-looking tarantula. But there are several types of spiders and insects that people enjoy keeping as pets. Insects and spiders can be fascinating to watch. They are extremely quiet, clean pets that do not need much room to live and do not require vast amounts of care. However, they are fragile creatures that will not stand much handling. Tarantulas have delicate abdomens and can die from falling just a short distance. In addition, many spiders, as well as some insects and scorpions, are poisonous. If you are sitting for one of these creatures, make sure the client tells you how you can keep yourself safe from injury. If you are allergic to bee or wasp venom, you might have an anaphylactic reaction to stings from these insects as well. Always wash your hands after handling these pets or their cages; poisons or irritating hairs can make you sick.

These pets eat a variety of foods, depending on the species. Some spiders and insects require special feeding. Hissing cockroaches tend to eat easy-to-find fruits and vegetables, but tarantulas need special prey. Tarantulas will eat crickets, moths, beetle larvae, houseflies and cockroaches. Larger tarantulas eat mice and small birds in the wild. Tarantulas should not be fed a prey food larger than half their own size. Leaf and stick insects, such as walking sticks and praying mantis, eat fresh vegetation. An ant farm is simple to care for, since the farm only needs feeding once a week with a little piece of sugary bread. Many of these pets will require food only once or twice a week. If you are caring for one of these creatures, make sure you understand exactly how much to feed, and when the pet should be fed.

Each type of insect has a specific habitat that you will need to learn to maintain while sitting for the pet. Make sure you have all the supplies for these insects, as it may be more difficult to find a source for special scorpion peat than it is to find specialty dog food if you run out. Some insects, such as praying mantis or walking sticks, can be hard to see as their defense mechanism is designed to help them blend in with the environment. Other insects have wings and can easily escape their cage when you are caring for them. Always do a visual check to be sure one of these pets has not gotten loose.

Sugar Gliders

Sugar gliders are small Australian marsupials similar to flying squirrels. They have furry membranes that extend from their wrists to their ankles that allow them to glide through the air. Sugar gliders are social creatures that crave companionship. They bond well with their owners if they receive the attention they need. Caring for a sugar glider can be time-consuming due to their need for attention. For this reason, some owners have more than one so that they can keep each other company.

Sugar gliders are nocturnal and will be most active at night. You may want to schedule your pet sitting appointment during the hours they are most active, though they will be happy to spend time with their owners during the day.

These pets have an exotic diet in the wild, but pet owners feed them a combination of insects, worms, small chopped fruits, and boiled eggs. The pet owner may mix up food ahead of time or have you prepare the food each day. Be sure to clean out any uneaten food each day and thoroughly clean the food and water bowls. Make sure the sugar glider has a source of clean water at all times.

Owners keep sugar gliders in a cage large enough for the animals to jump and run around in. A tree stump, cage platforms, and some toys will keep them occupied. Sugar gliders have been known to figure out how to unlock a cage and let themselves out; you need to make sure the cage is secure. Sugar gliders appreciate a nest area, which may be a box, a hammock, or a clay pot to snuggle into. Owners often provide cloth rags for the gliders to use as bedding material.

Sugar gliders may appear delicate or fragile, but they are hardy creatures with few health problems as long as they are properly cared for. They do suffer from back leg paralysis, which experts believe is due to a vitamin deficiency. Many veterinarians may not have the expertise to treat sugar gliders; if your client has not found a veterinarian that specializes in these creatures, you can call a specialty pet store or find a contact through the Internet.

Wallabies

Wallabies are wild Australian marsupials sometimes called "miniature kangaroos." Owners in the United States sometimes need a special permit to keep wallabies. Wallabies live between 12 and 15 years, weigh from 35 to 40 pounds, and reach about two and one-half feet tall. They are nocturnal in the wild but will adapt to their owners' schedule in captivity.

Wallabies eat raw fruits and vegetables, grass, wheat bread, and a formulated wallaby food that supplies necessary vitamins and nutrition. Wallabies are clean animals that require a ready supply of clean water.

In temperate climates, wallabies are hardy enough to live outside in a fenced yard with shelter (such as a dog house), but in cold climates they are indoor pets. They can be paper-trained, but any accidents are easily cleaned as they drop small pellets as stool. If they are kept outside, they should be protected from predators such as dogs or coyotes.

Hand-raised wallabies are gentle creatures, but those caught in the wild will be difficult to tame. Tame wallabies are inquisitive and affectionate but can be skittish. Do not make sudden moves or approach them too quickly.

Wild Animals

Some pet owners have rescued woodland creatures — raccoons, opossums, squirrels, and rabbits. While trying to raise wild creatures as pets is a difficult job, it can be done. Make sure you understand local regulations about keeping wild animals before you agree to take a client with any of these creatures.

Many of these animals are nocturnal, and it will be difficult to change their habits. The owner will likely keep them in a cage. Raccoons and squirrels are especially adept at finding their way out of cages and rooms. Their diet should be similar to the foods they would eat in the wild. Raccoons, skunks, and opossums are omnivorous. Rabbits are herbivores, and squirrels eat fruits, seeds, and nuts. Be sure you understand the food requirements and schedules of the type of animal you will be sitting for. All of these animals require fresh food and water, but raccoons especially need a squeaky-clean cage and a plentiful supply of clean water to wash their food.

If a client calls you to tell you that he or she has found an injured animal and asks for advice, offer to help find a wildlife rehabilitation expert. This is a better choice than trying to raise a wild animal that may grow up and behave unpredictably, and that will be unable to return to its natural environment.

Farm Animals

Sitters experienced in caring for farm animals and livestock may find themselves in demand at local farms when a farmer needs a break. Large ranching and farming operations typically have the staff to cover someone's absence, but a small farmer may need a hand when they are sick or need to go on a trip. It is important not to oversell your skills to a farmer. There are big differences between house pets and farm animals, and an inexperienced caretaker can cause damage and loss of property.

With the exception of horses, farm animals are not primarily pets. A sitter should always keep in mind that animals raised for meat, fur, wool, or milk are different than animals raised for companionship. These animals can show affection and be personable, but the sitter should always treat the animals as semi-wild creatures.

When you are caring for barn animals, your chores will likely include feeding the animals hay and grain, cleaning stalls or paddocks, putting down fresh bedding, grooming the animals, turning the animals out for exercise, and putting on or removing blankets. In cold climates, you might also need to shovel access areas and crack the ice in troughs or buckets. These appointments will typically take longer than a 30-minute house pet visit — an hour or longer, depending on the number and species of animals. For that reason, your rates might be much higher than a typical dog appointment.

Be especially cautious of your safety when caring for livestock. You will typically work with larger animals that may become skittish. You might also need to lift heavy objects. Make sure you lift with your legs and not with your back. If you are injured you cannot keep your other appointments.

You must double check doors, gates, and fences. Make sure the animals' food sources are securely locked; animals that get into their grain stores can gorge themselves to death. If a gate or door is accidentally left open, trying to herd animals back into their pens can be a frustrating, time-consuming job. There are several ways to get the animals back where they belong. In your initial interview with the client, ask him or her about the herding and feeding noises the animals are accustomed to. By using these signals, or by making feeding sounds such as clanging their feed buckets, the animals may come back on their own. You can also set out some feed to get the animals into their pens.

If a group of animals has escaped, they will likely follow what everyone else is doing. Walk behind the herd or flock, push them in the right direction by prodding them with a guide, and shout commands that will turn them away from you and back where they belong. Watch out for rebels that want to set their own direction. Go after those wanderers before they influence the rest of the group. If you are all alone and there is a danger that the animals may wander onto a road, call for help. If a herd becomes agitated or spooked, be careful. You could be trampled or crushed in the chaos.

When caring for herd animals, it can be easy to see if an animal is having a problem. Look for normal behavior, and the abnormal will stick out like a sore thumb. An animal that isolates itself from the flock, paces in circles, or chews on itself or others is an animal to watch. Livestock are animals that spend time each day running around outside, and they may wound themselves. The closer a wound is to the animal's heart, the more serious the injury is. Leg wounds are of particular concern. If the injury is not severe, clean the wound but do not wrap it; the animal will pick it off anyway. Livestock is an expensive investment; if in doubt about an animal's health, call a veterinarian.

Horses

A horse's digestive system is made to process large quantities of grass, which is high in fiber and water. The basic diet for most horses should be grass and quality hay. In most cases, plenty of fresh, clean water should be available at all times, even if the horse only drinks once or twice a day.

Most of the time, horses should be able to graze or eat hay when they want. An empty stomach lends itself to a higher risk of ulcers — quite common in race and sport horses. How much to feed depends on various factors, such as condition and activity level, but most horses should eat between 2 percent and 4 percent of their body weight in pounds of hay or other feed.

When you arrive at your sitting appointment, make sure there are plenty of piles of manure. This signals a well-functioning digestive system. Also check the horse's water bucket. A healthy horse should drink between 25 and 30 gallons of water each day.

As social animals, horses enjoy interaction with other horses and the company of humans. They will prick their ears up to hear you talk. They enjoy being petted and scratched around the head, shoulders, and hindquarters. Do not move suddenly toward the horse, and allow it to smell your hand before you pet it. If the client allows you to feed the horse treats, such as apples or carrots, hold your hand flat so that the horse can lift it off your palm. Because of the placement of their eyes, they cannot distinguish your fingers from the food.

Horses were born to move. In the wild, they may walk many miles in a day. They sometimes trot, but rarely gallop unless they have to. Daily opportunity to exercise is a must. Horses are easily spooked, skittish animals. Approach them deliberately and slowly, and keep talking to them. If you have to pass behind a horse, put a hand on its hindquarters as you are crossing behind it. This helps the horse know where you are. Horses defend themselves by kicking out; if you are crossing behind a horse getting ready to kick, the closer you are to the leg, the less injured you will be.

Horses signal upset by shaking their heads back and forth, showing the whites of their eyes, baring their teeth, and laying their ears back against their heads. A horse might make a mock nip at you before biting for real. Pay attention to these signs, back away, and give the horse time to calm down if it is upset. Do not remain in a stall with an agitated horse. You could be badly hurt.

If your client has asked you to groom the horse, tie the horse loosely to a railing to prevent the horse from wandering off. With a soft-bristled brush, brush the horse's forelock and face, being careful to stay away from the eyes. Look for any drainage from the eyes, and make sure the horse's ears do not have anything in them. Use a medium-bristled brush on the horse's body. Start at the neck, and work your way down. As you brush, look for any cuts or bumps that need treatment and for any swelling on the horse's legs. You may also want to check that any fly bites have not started to fester on the horse's skin. Use a stiff-bristled brush for the mane and tail. If required, use a hoof pick to clean out each hoof. While you are doing so, check for abscesses or other abnormalities.

Signs of sickness might be a discharge from the horse's nose or eyes, white or yellow gums, or lethargic behavior. A sick horse may be uninterested in food or may not be producing any droppings. They may repetitively get up and lie down or may roll around on the ground. A hurt leg is commonly signaled by lifting the leg or favoring it when walking. If you see a horse sweating profusely, trembling, or biting at its sides, the horse may have serious stomach problems. Any of these problems warrant a call to a veterinarian.

Case Study: Teresa Lewis

Teresa Lewis

Helping Hands Animal Care

Chesapeake, Virginia

Horses can be fun but challenging to care for. One horse that I watched knew I kept horse treats in my pocket. I brought him in for the evening to put him in his stall and feed him. He knew I had treats and kept stepping on my feet. The third time my boot came off and I stepped right in a pig pile of horse droppings with my sock.

He still had the nerve to try and eat my pocket to get his treats. I took care of three horses that had specific feeding times. When I put the horses in their stalls, they would rattle their buckets until I put some sweet feed in them, and then all was well. They were particular about their food!

Case Study: Teresa Lewis

Another time I was caring for a quarter horse named Stuart. I had bought a bag of apples that nobody would eat, and then I went and bought gourmet apples. I thought I could pawn off the lower-quality apples on Stuart and not waste them, and he spit them out. He would not eat the cheap apples, but when I gave him a gourmet apple, he gobbled it up!

Cattle

Depending on the type of cattle, and the stage of the animal's life cycle, cows, bulls, steers, and calves may be separated from each other. It is important to follow the client's instructions if the animals are segregated.

Cows have less-sensitive digestion systems than horses; therefore cattle are often fed lesser-quality hay. They may also be fed a portion of silage, a fermented mixture of grains and hay. If the client has both horses and cows, be sure to keep the silage away from the horses. Cattle may be kept inside a barn, or they may range free in a pasture. In either case, they should always have access to water.

A farmer client may ask you to brush the cow, especially if it is a show breed. They may ask you to milk it if it is a dairy cow. Do not agree to care for animals that require milking unless you already know what to do. Make sure you know where the tools and supplies are before you begin taking care of the animal.

Cows are fairly placid creatures, but they can get jumpy. If a cow lowers its head and points its crown at you or paws the ground, it may be ready to butt you. Back away quickly and carefully.

Cows sleep lying down, but a cow lying down in the same position for a long time, perhaps eight to 12 hours, may have a serious problem. Call a veterinarian.

Sheep and Goats

Goats and sheep are increasingly being kept as pets and as flock that produce meat, wool, and milk. Many people prefer the miniature breeds of goats for pets, while regular-sized breeds are used as livestock. There are a few miniature breeds of sheep. These are herd animals that tend to choose a leader and follow its behavior. If you find the leader, you might be able to use its authority to guide the flock. While these animals are easy to handle and respond well to human attention, goats are more energetic, creative, and inquisitive. If they can find a way out of a pen, they will do so. Sheep are more timid but will tend to follow the flock; if one gets out the rest will too.

Equally important in containing goats and sheep is keeping predators out. Goats and sheep are prey animals, and are vulnerable to attacks by predators such as dogs and coyotes. If the neighbors have pet dogs, make sure the dogs do not pose a danger to the flock. Most pet dogs possess a natural predatory instinct. Even if dogs do not attack a sheep or goat, they can cause stress and trauma.

Your client will likely provide hay for the flock and will occasionally offer grain or a special sheep or goat feed. Most owners also allow the animals time to forage for grass, clover, weeds, hay, briars, and shrubs. Sheep are grazers and prefer to eat weeds, grass, and clover, whereas goats are browsers. They will eat grass, but prefer to eat woody plants, shrubs, trees, and leaves. Keep them away from common poisonous landscaping plants such as rhododendrons. Goats and sheep will eat plants that many other livestock refuse. They must always have a supply of clean water. Unlike cattle, goats and sheep will not drink dirty water. If they are getting sufficient moisture from their feed, they may not drink much fresh water.

Both of these animals are a member of the ruminant group, which means that they must regurgitate and chew the cud over again. This, combination with their four-part stomach system, makes them susceptible to gas bloat. They may nip at their sides with this pain. Some owners treat the animals' gas problems with the over-the-counter human remedy Gas-X®; ask the owner if he or she has such a remedy at hand. An additional area of concern is when a sheep gets tipped over on its back. It may have a hard time turning over, which can lead to a serious buildup of gas. Always check the herd and count the animals to be sure they are doing well and that none have wandered off.

Sheep and goats commonly receive exercise by wandering in a paddock, pasture, or pen during the day. At night, the animals are often put in a barn. Goats and sheep should have protection from extreme weather conditions; there must be a way for them to get out of the rain, snow, or wind. Goats do not like to get wet and will seek shelter more quickly than sheep and other livestock. The shelter should be kept dry to prevent hoof disease or other problems.

If a sheep or goat is not feeling well, it may isolate itself and stop eating. It will hang its head down. Its ears and tail may droop. Teeth grinding is a sign of pain. Call a veterinarian if you see these signs.

Chickens, Ducks, Geese, Turkeys, and Doves

Chickens, ducks, and other poultry are popular barnyard animals to provide meat and eggs. They can live anywhere from five to ten years depending on the quality of life provided. Most hens stop laying eggs around three years of age. A baby chick requires special care in the first four weeks. They will need starter food and an enclosure with warming lights. After four weeks of age, they can move from their baby box to an adult cage.

For the first four weeks, owners provide a draft-free shallow wooden box with a screened lid. They often line the box with pine shavings about one inch deep. When you are caring for these chicks, the lining should be changed daily or as needed when wet. Warmth is the key to keeping the birds happy and healthy. Temperatures should be about 90° to 95° F. for the first week and lowered by five degrees each week until they are four weeks old.

After four weeks, the birds are ready roam around outside and have access to the adult cage sleeping quarters. Make sure the birds are tucked into the sleeping quarters — preferably with a door — at night, away from drafts and predators.

Farmyard birds eat chicken or duck food found at any local feed store. As the chicks get bigger, they will require a change in diet from a starter diet to a growth diet. They may also require different diets during their molting periods or laying periods. Always provide easy access to water and grit which helps in the digestion of their food.

Common problems can include upper respiratory infections and impaction. The signs of infection are runny eyes and nose, or crusty eyes and nose. A bird that isolates itself, or acts lethargic or clumsy, may also have a problem that requires a veterinarian.

Birds have many natural enemies. Protect your client's flock from dogs, cats, coyotes, and hawks. Be sure to keep an eye on the animals whenever they are roaming free in the yard. It is also not a good idea to keep two chickens together unless they are the same age and size, because the bigger of the two will peck the other causing injury. Poultry are not aggressive to humans, but they may peck or claw an enemy when agitated.

Pigs

Pigs are considered one of the smartest mammals, which can make them affectionate, crafty, and challenging. Pigs can grow to 300 pounds or larger, and they are formidable creatures. Pigs can figure out ways to escape pens, or get into anything they find interesting.

Some farmers raise their pigs in a pen or a barn, while others let the pigs roam a pasture. Young pigs will stay where the food is, while mature pigs will forage and explore. Pig barns often have a sloping floor that leads to a drain for easy cleaning. You may need to daily hose down or scrape the manure out of the enclosure and into a bin, and you should lay down fresh straw each day as bedding.

The client will likely provide a grain or pellet mixture for feeding along with small amounts of hay; some owners also feed the pig table scraps. Pigs can become aggressive when hungry; be sure to feed them promptly. They need fresh water both for drinking and cooling, especially in the summer. Pigs enjoy a mud bath in the summer to protect the skin from sunburn and to cool themselves.

When feeding and cleaning the pen, take the time to give them some attention. They appreciate having their backs scratched and may even let you scratch their bellies. Be cautious around pigs with a litter, as the mother can become defensive or territorial.

One indication that a pig is sick is that it refuses to eat. Another sign is that its hair might stick out all over its body. A pig that is wheezing, coughing, or has discharge from the mouth or eyes should be treated by a veterinarian.

Llamas and Alpacas

These fascinating, gentle animals originated in the mountains of South America, where they served as pack animals, provided food, and were prized for their wool. Alpacas in particular have extremely fine, silky hair used to make beautiful woolens. These animals are related to camels, but are not strong enough to carry humans. At 250 to 450 pounds, llamas are larger than alpacas, which grow to 100 to 175 pounds.

Farmers still raise these animals for wool, and they can be a valuable herd, because they are hardy, docile, not easily frightened, and easily cared for. They are also valuable as guard animals for other flocks, such as sheep, chickens, and geese.

Llama and alpaca feeding practices are similar to those for sheep. Llamas and alpacas are adaptive feeders, eating grasses, forbs, shrubs, and trees. They can be kept on a variety of pastures and hay. However, you must take care that they are not exposed to poisonous plants in the pasture area. Check with your client to be sure the grazing area is safe before agreeing to care for these animals. Some farmers feed the animals supplemental grain, such as small alfalfa pellets, cracked corn, or rolled oats. If pellets are fed, they should be mixed with a coarse feed or spread out in a large pan, because llamas frequently choke on the pellets. These animals should always have a supply of fresh, clean water.

Llamas and alpacas can be attacked by predators, such as dogs or coyotes, and they are able to jump a standard four to five-foot fence if threatened. These are loyal pack animals who become agitated if one is separated from the crowd. Farmers will house them in one communal pen, which should be secured from predators before you leave the sitting appointment. The animals tend to pick one area for a group manure pile, which makes your cleanup job easier. Llamas are fastidious animals; you will need to clean the manure during each visit.

Signs of sickness might include drooling, muscle stiffness, or discharge from the nose and eyes. Like most animals, signs of lethargy or isolation are signals that something may be wrong, and a veterinarian should be called.

Barn Cats

It is likely that as you work a sitting appointment on a farm you will encounter barn cats. These cats may be semi-wild, feral or simply outdoor pets. Farmers have traditionally kept cats on the farm to keep the mice, bird, and rabbit population down. Barn cats are not the same as house cats. They may or may not allow themselves to be petted, and they might be unpredictable. Ask your client if he or she feeds these animals any kind of pet food or if the cats rely on foraging and hunting other animals. Barn cats will find their own nesting areas and drink from the same water supply as the livestock. You should be careful not to let barn cats into the home.

Your client may not want you to take special care of these cats, but it does not hurt to ask about their wishes. However, if you see a barn cat hurt or obviously sick, you have an obligation to help.

"We can judge the heart of a man by his treatment of animals."

~ Immanual Kant"

Other Services

Your business is booming. Your clients are happy. Now it is time to explore offering more services.

You can provide new services to stand out from the other sitters in the area or simply to keep yourself from becoming caught up in a routine. You may want to get your clients to spend more money with you. You may see a need in your clients' lives that you are interested in filling. You may want to expand your business by including new types of work. Whatever your reasons, there are many ways you can add more value to your pet sitting services. Look for the needs in your current clients and in the area:

- What are you not providing?
- What tasks can you add to your roster of services without a huge investment?
- What classes or training would you need to provide expanded services?
- Do you have the time it takes to learn the new jobs and to publicize the new offerings?

Case Study: Terri Randall

Terri Randall

Creature Comforts Pet Care

Sheridan, Wyoming

I am certified in pet first aid, cardiopulmonary resuscitation (CPR), and other medical care. I have a number of special needs pets, such as diabetics that need injections.

I am educated and comfortable in handling these special pets. I am also currently working on my certification in canine massage and will offer that after fully certified. I offer overnight care under special circumstances as well as pet taxi services for pets for their vet or groomer appointments.

Expanded Home Services

One area of expansion could be including extra services while you are sitting. For example, you might offer shoveling snow, weeding gardens, mowing lawns, and watering yard — for an extra fee. If you do not already offer plant care, you can add that to your roster of services. Beyond watering the plants, you might mist the plants, polish flat-leaved plants such as philodendrons, or rotate them in sunlight. Make sure you have complete and specific instructions on caring for plants, just as you would for a pet. Some rare plants can be both sensitive and expensive.

You may agree to stay at the home for an appliance or maintenance call. People may need this service if they are at work during the day and cannot take time off for an appointment, or if the service is in conjunction with a regular pet sitting appointment while the client is out-of-town. This can be a boon to the client, since repair personnel do not always have hours convenient for people who work all day. If you are asked to stay for a maintenance call, make sure you are authorized to sign off on the work, and be sure the work is paid for ahead of time. If you are asked to authorize extra charges, let the client make that decision.

While you should clean up any messes that the animals make, clean cages, and wash their food and water bowls each day, you might also offer more extensive cleaning for an extra charge. The client might love coming home to a fresh, sparkling house that has been dusted, scrubbed, and mopped. You might clean the pets' blankets or sleeping pads, do the laundry, or vacuum the home. If you do not mind cleaning, this is an excellent way to add income while spending additional time with lonely pets. However, if you hate dusting and mopping, this is a service you may choose not to offer.

You can also offer to do grocery shopping so that the client comes home to a well-stocked refrigerator. Pet sitters may sometimes need to pick up extra food or cat litter when the client is gone, but shopping for the client is another task that you should charge for. Although this is not specifically related to pet sitting, you may want to offer this to your clients. You might consider this a "personal assistant" type of role. It may even be a convenient stop between appointments, but it could also be a task that takes time away from your pet sitting jobs. If you offer this, make sure you receive money in advance to pay for the groceries, and add a surcharge for your time, mileage, and effort.

Dogs that are cooped up for long periods of time become anxious, hyper, and destructive out of boredom. For this reason, clients who work long hours may hire you to make a midday visit to their dogs for exercise or for crate-training a puppy. A client may ask you to take the dog to a puppy play group if the pet is compatible with other dogs. Horse owners may need someone to be present when a farrier comes to shoe and care for the hooves of their animals. Other pet owners may need a sitter to taxi their pet to a veterinarian visit — an opportunity to promote your business to the veterinarian's office.

Obedience Training

Sitters with experience in obedience-training dogs are in high demand. Not only does the animal receive love, exercise, and daily care, but the client can come home to a dog that has been trained not to bark, to come when it is called, not to jump up on humans or lay on furniture, not to bite or chew on furniture, and to stay in place when he or she is told. Sitters with this experience can help crate-train a puppy or work on housebreaking the animal. This service might be performed during a pet sitting appointment while the client is out of town or during regular midday visits while the client is at work.

Dogs are pack animals that are used to following a leader. As the trainer establishes leadership, the dog will respond to commands. Positive reinforcement works especially well. After training has begun, the trainer or pet sitter should show the client all the words and rewards used for the training so the owner can continue the training after the appointment.

Many dog trainers learn training techniques by training their own dogs or by taking a basic obedience class and applying those principles to their animals. You may want to sample different obedience classes to find the techniques that fit your style the best and then adapt the principles into a course most comfortable for you. The American Kennel Club™ (AKC) offers programs and certifications, and the Association of Pet Dog Trainers (APDT) is another excellent resource. Joining a local dog club will offer learning experiences and a new market for your pet sitting services. Even if you do not offer obedience training at each appointment, the training skills will help you manage any dog.

Pet Grooming

As your skills and experience increase, you may want to offer in-home pet grooming services to your clients. Depending on the species and breed, grooming could include bathing the pet; brushing and clipping the coat; clipping nails, teeth, or wings; removing tear stains from fur; cutting out matted fur; expressing anal glands; flea and tick removal; or treating the animal's skin. Pet grooming requires special tools such as clippers, scissors, brushes, nail trimmers, and special shampoos and ointments.

Providing in-home grooming is different than providing services at a grooming store. You will need to take your tools with you and adapt to the conditions in the home. Some mobile groomers have a van completely outfitted to roll into the client's driveway and perform grooming from the van. This requires a considerable outlay of money, but for those with the inclination and the working capital this can be a rewarding venture.

When grooming animals it is important to pay attention to disinfecting of tools and the grooming area. If you treat an animals for fleas or mites, be sure you are not spreading these to the next animal on your sitting schedule. Wash your hands thoroughly with antibacterial soap before caring for the next animal.

Sitters should complete professional grooming training, or gain experience by working in a pet groomer's before offering grooming services. The following organizations provide information about breed grooming certification and guidance on how to charge appropriately for your services.

- NDGAA
  National Dog Groomers Association of America, Inc.
  Telephone contact: 724-962-2711
  www.nationaldoggroomers.com

- ISCC
  International Society of Canine Cosmetologists
  E-mail contact: iscc@petstylist.com
  www.petstylist.com

- IPG
  International Professional Groomers, Inc.
  Telephone contact: 847-758-1938
  www.ipgcmg.org

Other associations may be listed at **www.PetGroomer.com** in the Yellow Pages.

Pet Products

Some pet sitters also promote and sell products specific to the pets in which they specialize. This could include specialized foods or meal supplements, leashes, toys, clothing, or hygiene products. If you want to sell products, be sure you have room in your home for inventory. Price your products so that you will make enough profit to benefit your business, and be prepared to show your clients why your products are the best for their pets.

Hobbies or outside interests can also help you offer additional services or products to pet lovers. If you are someone who likes to knit, sew, or craft, you might begin knitting sweaters or other articles of clothing for pets in cold climates. Some pet owners love to dress their pets up for Halloween, and a seamstress can make money creating custom costumes for animals. Seamstresses can personalize pet blankets by sewing the name of the pet or embroidering blankets and other possessions with designs of the owner's choice.

Fabric pet carriers for miniature dog breeds and other small pets have become popular because some pet owners love to carry their pets with them. With good sewing skills and good marketing techniques, a sitter could branch out into the carrier and handbag business. A business owner who loves photography can offer photo shoot sessions with the pet and family; if a sitter loves scrap booking, he or she could create special memory books for pet lovers.

Pet Bakery

Some pet sitters expand their businesses by offering homemade pet treats. Here are a few recipes to try. Even if you do not sell these you might offer them to the pets you care for. You may create a demand for your treats, and you could begin to market them online or sell them through the mail.

Homemade Dog Biscuits

- 1 tablespoon (or 1 package) dry yeast
- 3 1/2 cup unbleached flour
- 1 cup cornmeal
- 1 egg
- 3 1/2 cups lukewarm chicken broth
- 2 cup whole wheat flour
- 1/2 cup skim milk powder

Preheat oven to 300° F. Dissolve the yeast in the lukewarm chicken broth. Let the yeast broth mixture set 10 minutes. Mix together the flours and cornmeal and pour into the yeast mixture. Roll resulting dough out 1/4" thick. Cut dog biscuit shapes from dough.

Mix together skim milk powder and egg. Brush biscuits with egg wash. Bake on greased cookie sheets for 45 minutes. Then turn off oven and leave in overnight to finish hardening. Makes 60 medium-sized biscuits.

Kitten Cookies

- 1 cup whole wheat flour
- 1 teaspoon catnip
- 1/3 cup skim milk
- 1/3 cup powdered milk
- 2 tablespoon butter, vegetable oil, or canola oil
- 1/4 cup soy flour
- 1 egg
- 2 tablespoon wheat germ
- 1 tablespoon unsulfured molasses

Preheat oven to 350° F. Mix dry ingredients together. Add molasses, egg, oil and milk. Roll out flat onto oiled cookie sheet and cut into small, cat bite-sized pieces. Bake for 20 minutes. Let cool and store in tightly sealed container.

Homemade Bird Balls

- 1 pound of lard
- 5 cups corn meal
- 2 cups sunflower seeds
- 1 jar of peanut butter
- 6 cups oats
- 2 cups raisins

Mix all ingredients except sunflower seeds and raisins together. Roll into 5 or 6 small balls. Roll balls in sunflower seeds and raisins. Place the balls in a bird feeder or bird's food dish. These also make delicious treats for wild birds. Just place the treat on a feeder, a deck rail, or in a suet feeder.

Maintenance Contracts

Another area for expansion is in contracting your services to offices, doctors, restaurants, and other places that keep aquariums or other pets on display. You can offer cleaning, maintenance, and weekend visits to these places, especially if there is no staff in the building on the weekends.

You may need special equipment for these jobs, especially if you are working with larger aquariums. Such a job might also require you to learn more about fish and aquarium animal health, and you may need to supply special chemicals. For a sitter with extensive experience in caring for fish, this could be an ideal business expansion.

Conclusion

For animal lovers, there are few jobs more satisfying than caring for pets. The daily variety and the challenge can keep pet sitters eager to go to work each day. Having a job where your coworkers — four-legged ones — are eager to see you and love your attention can cheer up any sitter's day.

With hard work, honesty, and attention to details, your dream of owning a successful pet sitting business is within your reach. Cultivate your clients carefully and always do your best. News of your good care will spread through your community. Remember to always uphold the ethics of the pet sitting profession. You are the ambassador of pet sitting to anyone you meet.

"If you can dream it, you can be it."

"It is impossible to keep a straight face in the presence of one or more kittens."

~Cynthia E Varnado

Appendix A: Helpful Resources

There are many organizations, associations, and charities that can help you in your quest to become a top-notch pet sitter. Some of the resources mentioned here will help you gain skills and experience with animals; others will provide you with support, networking opportunities, and client contacts. The information here is up-to-date as of the publish date of this book; check with your local library, the Internet, or the organizations themselves for any new information.

Organizations for Pet Sitters

Pet Sitters International (PSI™)

www.petsit.com

Pet Sitters International is dedicated to educating professional pet sitters and promoting, supporting, and recognizing excellence in pet sitting. This professional association offers pet sitters an accreditation program to sharpen their professional skills. An in-depth educational program teaches pet sitters all they need to know about pet care, health and nutrition, business management, office procedures, and additional services. The top pet-sitting professionals in the industry have worked together to develop this coursework.

Professional United Petsitters LLC

www.petsits.com

This organization offers support, resources, and pet sitting business start-up kits to members. The membership kit contains the following materials:

- Public business listing on the **www.petsits.com** sitter directory
- Membership to forums and links boards
- An e-mail forwarding alias of your choice @petsits.com
- Free consultation or form customization and logo insertion
- Professional, customizable pet sitting, dog walking, pet care business forms and marketing materials
- Budgeting, mileage, financial, estimating, and scheduling tool workbooks
- Pet sitting information: marketing, Web site, start-up, and other guides
- List of more than 75 pet service directory listing sites and other money-saving pet supply links
- Pet recipes to share with clients or to add pet bakery items to your business

- Optional Web-ready service request system so that you can customize, upload, and receive requests via e-mail

National Association of Professional Pet Sitters (NAPPS)

www.petsitters.org

The National Association of Professional Pet Sitters is a nonprofit organization whose mission is:

- To provide tools and support to foster the success of members' businesses
- To promote the value of pet sitting to the public
- To advocate the welfare of animals

NAPPS offers its members professional integrity and education, as well as networking opportunities. In addition, the organization serves as a major voice for the pet sitting industry.

ARK Online

www.arkonline.com

ARK Online is an independent publication staffed by a group of people who care about animals and use the Web to broadcast information about animal welfare to readers.

American Society for the Prevention of Cruelty to Animals® (ASPCA®)

www.aspca.org

The ASPCA® is a nonprofit organization founded in 1866 as the first humane organization in the Western Hemisphere. The Society was formed to alleviate the injustices animals faced to continue to battle cruelty against animals.

The Humane Society of the United States

www.hsus.org

The Humane Society of the United States is the nation's largest and most effective animal protection organization. It provides information and care tips on all types of animals, current legislation regarding animals and pet owners, and resources for pet care.

American Kennel Club™ (AKC)

www.akc.org

The American Kennel Club™ is a nonprofit organization for purebred dogs whose activities include maintaining a purebred dog registry, sanctioning dog events, and an online store.

International Cat Association (TICA)

www.tica.org

The International Cat Association registers the pedigrees of all breeds of felines and catteries, licenses shows, establishes standards for all breeds, and provides information.

National Alternative Pet Association (NAPA)

www.altpet.net

The purpose of the National Alternative Pet Association is to preserve private ownership of exotic animals, including non-human primates.

Animal Fancy Rat and Mouse Association (AFRMA)

www.afrma.org

The American Fancy Rat and Mouse Association promotes and encourages breeding and exhibition of fancy rats and mice for show and as pets.

The American Ferret Association (AFA)

www.ferret.org

The American Ferret Association, Inc. promotes the domestic ferret as a companion and works to protect the domestic ferret against anti-ferret legislation, mistreatment, unsound breeding practices and overpopulation, and unnecessary scientific research.

American Pet Association (APA)

www.apapets.com

The American Pet Association is an independent, national humane organization dedicated to promoting responsible pet ownership through action, services and education.

American Rabbit Breeders Association, Inc. (ARBA)

www.arba.net

The American Rabbit Breeders Association is dedicated to the promotion, development, and improvement of the domestic rabbit and cavy industry.

Dog Age®

www.DogAge.com

Dog Age provides dog healthcare information, including information on canine diseases.

FelineDiabetes.com®

www.felinediabetes.com

FelineDiabetes.com® is a complete pet health guide to treatment of diabetes mellitus in cats.

The Pet Arthritis Resource Center

www.arthritis-cat-dogs.com

The Pet Arthritis Resource Center provides pet owners with information and research about animal arthritis.

VetInfo.com

www.vetinfo.com

The VetInfo Web site provides medical information for dogs and cats.

1-800-Save-A-Pet.com

www.1-800-Save-A-Pet.com

The 1-800-Save-A-Pet.com Web site helps link pet owners with pets that need homes.

Alley Cat Allies

www.alleycat.org

The Alley Cat Allies Web site is sponsored by The National Feral Cat Rescue, a national nonprofit clearinghouse for information on feral and stray cats.

Delta Society®

www.deltasociety.org

The Delta Society® is the leading international resource for service and therapy animals.

The International Hedgehog Association

www.hedgehogclub.com

The International Hedgehog Association works to educate the public in the care and betterment of hedgehogs.

National Dog Groomers Association of America, Inc. (NDGAA)

www.nationaldoggroomers.com

The NDGAA is an association of people engaged in the grooming and care of dogs. The association promotes excellence and professional standards in dog grooming.

National Fancy Rat Society (NFRS)

www.nfrs.org

The National Fancy Rat Society is a network of rat experts who promote the breeding and showing of rats along with education and show management.

National Gerbil Society (NGS)

www.gerbils.co.uk

The National Gerbil Society is a British society that works for the promotion of Gerbils and Jirds as pets and exhibition animals.

National Disaster Search Dog Foundation

www.searchdogfoundation.org

The National Disaster Search Dog Foundation provides information about the training of search and rescue teams.

People and Dogs Society (PADS)

www.padsonline.org

The People and Dogs Society is an organization dedicated to teaching responsible dog ownership.

Cats with No Name

www.catswithnoname.net

Cats with No Name is an organization dedicated to improving the health and welfare of homeless cats.

The Dog Rescues Network

www.dogrescues.net

The Dog Rescues Network provides a list of rescue organizations throughout the United States.

Doris Day Animal Foundation

www.ddaf.org

The Doris Day Animal Foundation is a lobbying organization focused on the humane treatment of animals.

The Hedgehog Welfare Society

www.hedgehogwelfare.org

The Hedgehog Welfare Society provides rescue, research, and education for people who care for hedgehogs.

The Senior Dogs Project

www.srdogs.com

The Senior Dogs Project provides information and support for older dogs.

Kitten Care

www.KittenCare.com

Kittencare.com is a Web site offering free tips and advice on taking care of cats.

The Cat Lover's Online Directory

www.KittySites.com

KittySites.Com offers links to information about cats and cat lovers.

The Dog Lover's Online Directory

www.PuppySites.com

PuppySites.Com offers links to information about dogs and dog lovers.

The Wolf Portal™

www.wolf.com

The Wolf Portal provides new and information about the preservation of wolves in the wild and the preservation of their native habitats.

World Wide Pet Industry Association, Inc.® (WWPIA®)

www.wwpsia.com

The WWPIA is a nonprofit trade association, which represents the companion animal and pet products industry: manufacturers, product distributors, breeder and livestock distributors, suppliers, manufacturers' representatives and retail businesses.

Animal Rescue and Charity Organizations

National Borzoi Rescue Foundation, Inc. (NBRF)

www.nbrf.info

The National Borzoi Rescue Foundation assists regional rescue groups and individuals in all aspects of Borzoi Rescue.

Operation Noble Foster

www.operationnoblefoster.org

Operation Noble Foster is an organization that links military personnel's pets with foster families.

Pet Guardian Angels of America™ (PGGA)

www.pgaa.com

The PGAA Web site is devoted to pets of all types. Their purpose is to help people select and care for pets and to assist in pet rescue.

Petfinder™

www.petfinder.com

The Petfinder™ Web site is a place where people can search for animals that need homes.

Shar Pei Savers, Inc.

www.sharpeisavers.com

Shar Pei Savers is a national dog rescue organization focused on Shar Pei dogs.

Online Networks

These free Internet groups are a way to interact and connect with other professional pet sitters, dog walkers, and dog daycare owners. Search **www.yahoo.com** to find each of these online groups.

- About Pet Sitting Yahoo Group
- Professional Pet Sitting Yahoo Group
- Online Network for Dog Daycare Owners
- Dog Daycare Yahoo Group
- North American Dog Daycare Association (NADDA) Yahoo Group

Regional Networks

These Yahoo groups are organized by region, and will put you in touch with other pet care professionals in your area.

Arizona

- Arizona Pet Sitter and Service Network

Arkansas

- League of Arkansas Professional Pet Sitters (LAPPS)

California

- Orange County — OC Pet Sitters
- San Diego County — The Pet Net
- Northern California Pet Sitters

- Peninsula Professional Pet Sitters

Florida

- Tampa Bay Professional Pet Sitters Network

Georgia

- Georgia Network of Professional Pet Sitters
- North Georgia Alliance of Professional Pet Sitters: A pet sitters networking group covering 19 counties in North Georgia.

Indiana

- Professional Pet Sitters of Indiana

Massachusetts

- Western Massachusetts Pet Sitters Network

Michigan

- Michigan Pet Sitters and Dog Walkers Association

Minnesota

- Professional Pet Sitters of Minnesota

Nebraska

- Omaha Pet Sitters Association

Nevada

- Southern Nevada Association of Professional Pet Sitters

New Mexico

- New Mexico Pet Sitters Alliance

New York

- Capital Area Professional Pet Sitters

North Carolina

- Charlotte Area Professional Pet Sitter's Network

Tennessee

- East Tennessee Association of Professional Pet Sitters

Texas

- Austin — Professional Pet Sitters of Austin
- Houston — Houston Area Professional Pet Sitters

Virginia

- Northern Virginia Professional Pet Sitters Network

Wisconsin

- Professional Pet Sitters Association of Wisconsin

Canada

- Canadian Pet Sitters and Dog Walkers
- Toronto Area Dog Walkers Alliance

Appendix B: Forms & Checklists

Sample Pet Sitting Contract

(COMPANY NAME) PET SITTING SERVICE CONTRACT

Contact Information

Note: If something does not apply to you or your home, please indicate by entering "N/A" in the space.

Name: ______________________________

E-mail address: ______________________________

Home Phone: ______________________________

Business Phone: ______________________________

Address: ______________________________

Who else has access to your home? Please write name and phone numbers.

Your Landlord: ______________________________

Maid/Cleaning Service: ______________________________

Other: ______________________________

Sample Pet Sitting Contract

Describe Your Pet(s)

If you have more than three pets, please attach additional information at bottom of sheet.

Pet's Name and species:

1) ______________________________

2) ______________________________

3) ______________________________

Sex:

1) ______________________________

2) ______________________________

3) ______________________________

Favorite toys/treats:

1) ______________________________

2) ______________________________

3) ______________________________

Number of visits per day: ______________________________

Please attach photos of each pet.

Sample Pet Information Form

Owner's name: ______________________

Home #: ______________________

Cell #: ______________________

Work #: ______________________

Address: ______________________

Designated Emergency Pet Guardian: ______________________

Home #: ______________________

Cell #: ______________________

Work #: ______________________

E-mail address: ______________________

Address: ______________________

Pet's name: ______________________

(circle one)

Dog Cat Other

Breed: ______________________ Age: __________

Sex: Male Female

Spayed/Neutered: Yes No

County Tag ID: ______________________

ID Microchip: Yes No

If yes, Microchip #: ______________________

Weight: ______________ Height: ______________

Eye color: ______________ Tail: ______________

Hair color: ______________ Hair length: ______________

Veterinarian Office: ______________________

Vet's Name: ______________________

Phone Number: ______________________

Sample Pet Information Form

Date of vaccinations: ______________________________

Any medical conditions/allergies: ______________________________

Any special medications? ______________________________

General disposition:

Is your pet good around children? Yes No

Is your pet good around dogs? Yes No

Is your pet good around cats? Yes No

Specific identifying marks and/or features that would help to ID your pet: ______________________________

List of people who could identify your pet:

1. Name: ______________________________

   Phone: ______________________________

2. Name: ______________________________

   Phone: ______________________________

General Pet Care Information

General Pet Care Information

PLEASE NOTE: The utmost care will be given in watching both your pet(s) and your home. However, due to the extreme unpredictability of animals, we cannot accept responsibility for any mishaps of any extraordinary or unusual nature (i.e. biting, furniture damage, and accidental death) or any complications in administering medications to the animal. Nor can we be liable for injury, disappearance, death or fines of pet(s) with access to the outdoors.

Vet Preference: ______________________________

Phone: ______________________________

Are pets secured in home or yard? :______________________________

Terms and Conditions

This is the contractual part; please fill in all the blanks and be sure to read carefully.

1. The parties herein agree as follows: The initial term of this contract shall be from_ ______________________________through______________________________

In the event of early return home, client must notify Pet Sitter promptly to avoid being charged for unnecessary visits(s).

2. The baseline fee is (hare per visit) x (number of visits) for a total $____________.

Other fees for additional services or circumstances may apply. Any additional visits made or services performed shall be paid for at the agreed contract rate. Pet Sitter is authorized to perform care and services as outlined on this contract. Pet Sitter is also authorized by Client (name entered below) to seek emergency veterinary care with release from all liabilities related to transportation, treatment, and expense.

3. Should specified veterinarian be unavailable, Pet Sitter is authorized to approve medical and/or emergency treatment (excluding euthanasia) as recommended by a veterinarian. Client agrees to reimburse Pet Sitter/Company for expenses incurred, plus any additional fee for attending to this need or any expenses incurred for any other home/food/supplies needed.

4. In the event of inclement weather or natural disaster, Pet Sitter is entrusted to use best judgment in caring for pet(s) and home. Pet Sitter/Company will be held harmless for consequences related to such decisions.

General Pet Care Information

5. Pet Sitter agrees to provide the services stated in this contract in a reliable, caring and trustworthy manner. Inconsideration of these services and as an express condition thereof, the client expressly waives and relinquishes any and all claims against said Pet Sitter/Company except those arising from negligence or willful misconduct the part of the Sitter/Company.

6. Client understands this contract also serves as an invoice and takes full responsibility for PROMPT payment of fees upon completion of services contracted. A finance charge of ___ percent per month will be added to unpaid balances after 30 days. A handling fee ($20) will be charged on all returned checks. One half deposit is required on lengthy assignments and first time clients or clients with a history of late payment and will be required to pay in advance before services are rendered. In the event it is necessary to initiate collection proceedings on the account, Client will be responsible for all attorney's fees and costs of collection.

7. In the event of personal emergency or illness of Pet Sitter, Client authorizes Pet Sitter to arrange for another qualified person to fulfill responsibilities as set forth in this contract. Client will be notified in such a case.

8. All pets are to be currently vaccinated. Should Pet Sitter be bitten or otherwise exposed to any disease or ailment received from Client's animal which has not been properly and currently vaccinated, it will be the client's responsibility to pay all costs and damages incurred by the victim.

9. Pet Sitter/Company reserves the right to terminate this contract at any time before or during its term. If Pet Sitter/Company, in its sole discretion, determines that Client's pet poses a danger to health or safety of Pet Sitter, if concerns prohibit Pet Sitter from caring for pet, Client authorizes pet to be placed in a kennel, with all charges there from to be charged to client.

10. Client authorizes this signed contract to be valid approval for future services of any purpose provided by this contract permitting Pet Sitter/Company to accept telephone reservations for service and enter premises without additional signed contracts or written authorization.

I have reviewed this Service Contract for accuracy and understand the contents of this form.

Date: ______________________________

Client: ______________________________

Pet Sitter/Company: ______________________________

Sample Animal Care Key Release Form

I authorize the representative of (Company Name) to use my house key(s) during the time he/she will be caring for my animals. If the animal sitter does not keep my key(s) on file after the first two series of visits, there will be a $5 charge to pick up and return them to me. Indicate before visits occur by checking the appropriate box:

☐ Please leave my key(s) inside my home after the last visit

☐ Please leave my key(s) ______________________________

☐ Please keep my key(s) for future visits until further notified.

☐ Please return my key(s) to me after my return in person

Signature______________________________

If you have not authorized the representative to keep your key(s) and we will be leaving them in your home or other place specified, please return this form with your check to verify that your key(s) are in your possession.

☐ My key(s) have been returned to me

Signature______________________________

Sample Veterinarian Notification

During my absence, a representative of our pet sitting service will be caring for my animal(s) and has my permission to transport them to your office for treatment. I authorize you to treat my animal(s) and will be responsible for payment upon my return or will leave my credit card number below for you to charge.

Please file this notification with my records.

Client______________________________ Date______________

Animal(s) Names____

____

____

Client signature____

Credit card type____

Credit card number______________________________________

Expiration date____

Sample Checklist for Clients

Your pet sitter is pleased to be given the responsibility for caring for your pet. To ensure the best for your pet's health and welfare while you are gone, we ask you to follow this checklist of items that will allow your pet sitter to provide top-notch care. As always, you can contact us with any questions.

- ☐ Provide documentation confirming that your pet is up-to-date on its shots. Make sure your pet wears current vaccination tags on its collar.
- ☐ If your pet chews on things, set out "chew toys" and do whatever is necessary to protect your personal items and home furnishings from his teeth while you are away.
- ☐ Write out your pet's favorite hiding places. This will help the sitter find your pet if he or she does not appear when the sitter arrives.
- ☐ If your pet has any unusual habits such as destructive behavior when left alone, change in bowel or eating habits, or others, tell your sitter about these in advance.
- ☐ If you own both dogs and cats, please note that the sitter is honor-bound to care for the cats as well. Please do not ask the sitter to ignore the cat in return for a lower rate.
- ☐ Set out everything your pet needs in one visible and accessible area. This includes food, treats, utensils, food and water bowls, medications, leash, can opener, toys, paper towels, cleaning supplies, garbage bags, litter and scoop, broom and dustpan and/or vacuum cleaner, pet towels, newspapers or other housebreaking materials, and watering can for plants.
- ☐ Provide extra food, litter, and supplies just in case you are home later than expected.
- ☐ Be sure to leave plastic bags for sanitary disposal of feces.
- ☐ Do not expect your sitter to pick up any pet messes that accumulated before their contract period.
- ☐ Clean out your refrigerator so that food does not spoil, and wash all dishes so that there is no chance of ants or other pests invading the house.
- ☐ Make sure the sitter knows how to pirate your heat and air conditioner, and which settings should be used for the comfort of your pet. Check your settings before you leave.

Sample Checklist for Clients

- ☐ Close off any areas of your home that are off limits to the pet or sitter, and let him or her know about it in advance. If there are any particular problems he or she should be aware of, such as a leaky faucet or a cat that likes to get into the garbage, tell him or her before you leave.
- ☐ If you are leaving anything specifically for your pet sitter, such as a batch of cookies or a tip, leave him or her a note. Sitters will not take anything from a house unless he or she is specifically invited to!
- ☐ If other people may access the house or care for the pets, make sure the sitter knows what he or she is responsible for and who he or she might encounter in the house. The sitter will not automatically know the difference between an authorized house visit and a break-in.
- ☐ Notify your veterinarian in writing that a pet sitter will be caring for your pet and authorize the veterinarian to extend medical care during your absence if needed.

Letter Requesting Payment of Overdue Bill

Dear (Client Name):

On reviewing our records, I have found that there is a delinquent balance on your account in the amount of $________. This balance is for pet sitting services provided by (sitter name) of (Company Name) from (dates of service). While this may just be an oversight on your part, we appreciate your prompt attention to this matter. We enjoy caring for your pets and would like to continue providing our services to you. For this reason, we ask that you remit payment to us within five (5) days.

Best Regards,

(Company Name)

Independent Pet Sitting Contractor Agreement

This Independent Contractor Agreement (the "Agreement") is entered into this [specify date] by and between [Name of Independent Contractor/Consultant] (the "Consultant"), a corporation located at [specify], d/b/a [specify], for itself and its heirs, executors, administrators, related entities and assigns and [Name of Company] (the "Company").

RECITALS

WHEREAS, the Company is in need of assistance in the area of (specify); and WHEREAS, Consultant has agreed to perform consulting work for the Company in (specify) services and other related activities for the Company;

NOW, THEREFORE, the parties hereby agree as follows:

1. Consultant's Services. Consultant shall be available and shall provide to the Company professional services in the area of (specify) ("Consulting Services") as needed and requested.

2. Consideration.

A. RATE. In consideration of the Services to be performed by Consultant under this Agreement the Company will pay Consultant the flat rate of (specify per job) or at the rate of (specify) per hour for time spent on Consulting Services. Consultant shall submit written, signed reports of the time spent performing Consulting Services, itemizing in reasonable detail the dates on which services were performed, the number of hours spent on such dates and a brief description of the services rendered. The Company shall pay Consultant the amounts due pursuant to submitted reports within (specify) after such reports are received by the Company.

B. EXPENSES. Additionally, the Company will pay Consultant for the following expenses (specify, such as: all travel expenses to and from all work sites; meal expenses; administrative expenses; lodging expenses if work demands overnight stays; and miscellaneous travel-related expenses including parking and tolls) incurred while this Agreement between Consultant and the Company exists.

Consultant shall submit written documentation and receipts where available itemizing the dates on which expenses are incurred. The Company shall pay Consultant the amounts due pursuant to submitted reports within (specify) after a report is received by the Company.

3. Independent Contractor. Nothing contained herein or any document executed in connection herewith, shall be construed to created an employer-employee partnership or joint venture relationship between the Company and Consultant. Consultant is an independent contractor and not an employee of the Company or any of

Independent Pet Sitting Contractor Agreement

its subsidiaries or affiliates. The consideration set forth in Section 2 shall be the sole consideration due Consultant for the services rendered hereunder. It is understood that the Company will not withhold any amounts for payment of taxes from the compensation of Consultant hereunder. Consultant will not represent to be or hold itself out as an employee of the Company and Consultant acknowledges that he/she shall not have the right or entitlement in or to any of the pension, retirement or other benefit programs now or hereafter available to the Company's regular employees. Any and all sums subject to deductions, if any, required to be withheld and/or paid under any applicable state, federal or municipal laws or union or professional guild regulations shall be Consultant's sole responsibility and Consultant shall indemnify and hold Company harmless from any and all damages, claims and expenses arising out of or resulting from any claims asserted by any taxing authority as a result of or in connection with said payments.

4. Confidentiality. In the course of performing consulting services, the parties recognize that Consultant may come in contact or become familiar with information which the Company or its subsidiaries or affiliates may consider confidential. This information may include, but is not limited to, information pertaining to (specify) which information may be of value to a competitor. Consultant agrees to keep all such information confidential and not to discuss or divulge it to anyone other than appropriate Company personnel or their designees.

5. Term. This Agreement shall commence on (specify date) and shall terminate on (specify date), unless earlier terminated by either party hereto. Either party may terminate this Agreement upon Thirty (30) days prior written notice. The Company may, at its option, renew this Agreement for an additional term of (specify) on the same terms and conditions as set forth herein by giving notice to Consultant of such intent to renew on or before (specify date).

6. Consultant's Taxpayer I.D. Number. The taxpayer I.D. number of the Consultant is (specify). The Consultant is licensed to perform the agreed upon services enumerated herein and covenants that it maintains all valid licenses, permits and registrations to perform same.

7. Insurance. The Consultant will carry general liability, automobile liability, workers' compensation and employer's liability insurance in the amount of (specify). In the event the Consultant fails to carry such insurance it shall indemnify and hold harmless Company, its agents and employees from and against any damages, claims, and expenses arising out of or resulting from work conducted by Consultant and its agents or employees.

8. Competent Work. All work will be done in a competent fashion in accordance with

Independent Pet Sitting Contractor Agreement

applicable standards of the profession and all services are subject to final approval by a representative of the Company prior to payment.

9. Representations and Warranties. The Consultant will make no representations, warranties, or commitments binding the Company without the Company's prior consent.

10. Legal Right. Consultant covenants and warrants that he/she has the unlimited legal right to enter into this Agreement and to perform in accordance with its terms without violating the rights of others or any applicable law and that he/she has not and shall not become a party to any other agreement of any kind which conflicts with this Agreement. Consultant shall indemnify and hold harmless the Company from any and all damages, claims and expenses arising out of or resulting from any claim that this Agreement violates any such agreements. Breach of this warranty shall operate to terminate this Agreement automatically without notice as specified in Paragraph 5 and to terminate all obligations of the Company to pay any amounts which remain unpaid under this Agreement.

11. The Waiver. Failure to invoke any right, condition, or covenant in this Agreement by either party shall not be deemed to imply or constitute a waiver of any rights, condition, or covenant and neither party may rely on such failure.

12. Enforceability. If any provision of this Agreement is held by a court of competent jurisdiction to be unenforceable, the reminder of the Agreement shall remain in full force and effect and shall in no way be impaired.

13. Miscellaneous.

a. Entire Agreement and Amendments. This Agreement constitutes the entire agreement of the parties with regard to the subject matter hereof, and replaces and supersedes all other agreements or understandings, whether written or oral. No amendment or extension of this Agreement shall be binding unless in writing and signed by both parties.

b. Binding Effect, Assignment. This Agreement shall be binding upon and shall inure to the benefit of Consultant and the Company and to the Company's successors and assigns. Nothing in this Agreement shall be construed to permit the assignment by Consultant of any of its rights or obligations hereunder, and such assignment is expressly prohibited without the prior written consent of the Company.

c. Governing Law, Severability. This Agreement shall be governed by the laws of the State of (specify). The invalidity or unenforceability of any provision of this Agreement shall not affect the validity or enforceability of any other provision.

Independent Pet Sitting Contractor Agreement

WHEREFORE, the parties have executed this Agreement as of the date written above.

COMPANY:

By: ______________________________

Date: ______________________________

CONSULTANT:

By: ______________________________

Date: ______________________________

Sample Employee Hiring Agreement

Date

Name of Employee

Address

City, State, Zip

Dear [Name of Employee]:

This letter confirms that [Name of Company] ("The Company") has hired you as its [specify title]. In consideration thereto, you agree to be employed under the following terms and conditions:

1. You agree to work full-time and use your best efforts while rendering services for the Company. As our [specify title], you will be responsible for: [specify in detail]

2. You will make no representations, warranties, or commitments binding the Company without our prior consent nor do you have any authority to sign any documents or incur any indebtedness on the Company's behalf.

3. You shall assume responsibility for all samples, sales literature and other materials delivered to you and you shall return same immediately upon the direction of the Company.

4. The company employs you at will and may terminate your employment at any time, without prior notice, with or without cause. Likewise, you are free to resign as our sales manager at any time, with or without notice.

5. The Company shall pay you a salary of [Specify $X] per [specify] as consideration for all services to be rendered pursuant to this Agreement. In addition, the Company shall provide you [enter any health, illness, vacation, holiday, or stock benefits here].

6. You agree and represent that you owe the Company the highest duty of loyalty. This means that you will never make secret profits at the Company's expense, will not accept kickbacks or special favors from Customers or Manufacturers, and will protect Company property.

7. While acting as an employee for the Company, you will not directly or indirectly, own an interest in, operate, control, or be connected as an employee, agent, independent contractor, partner, shareholder or principal in any company which markets products, goods or services which directly or indirectly compete with the business of the Company.

8. All lists, keys, and other records relating to the clients of the Company, whether

Sample Employee Hiring Agreement

prepared by you or given to you by the Company during the term of this Agreement, are the property of the Company and shall be returned immediately upon termination or resignation of your employment.

9. You further agree that for a period of Six (6) months following the termination or resignation of your employment, you shall not work for, own an interest in, or be connected with as an employee, stockholder or partner, any company which directly or indirectly competes with the business of the Company.

10. There shall be no change, amendment or modification of this Agreement unless it is reduced to writing and signed by both parties. This Agreement cancels and supersedes all prior agreements and understandings.

11. If any provision of this Agreement is held by a court of competent jurisdiction to be invalid or unenforceable, the remainder of the Agreement shall remain in full force and shall in no way be impaired.

Your signature in the lower left corner of this Agreement will indicate the acceptance of the terms and conditions herein stated.

Sincerely yours,

____

[specify Name and Title]

[NAME OF COMPANY]

("The Company")

I, [Name of Employee], the Employee stated herein, have read the above Agreement, understand and agree with its terms, and have received a copy.

____

[NAME OF EMPLOYEE]

Checklist of Startup Costs

Use this checklist to estimate and prepare for all the costs of starting up your business.

- ☐ Business License(s) Name Registration
  - ☐ Local
  - ☐ State
  - ☐ Federal
- ☐ Attorney Fees
  - ☐ Business Name Consultation and Registration
  - Legal Structure Costs (Partnership Agreement, Incorporation, and so on)
  - ☐ Business Form Development and Review Accountant Fees
- ☐ Insurance
  - ☐ Liability Insurance
  - ☐ Dishonesty Bond
  - ☐ Disability Income I
  - ☐ Automobile Umbrella Coverage Rent for Office Space
- ☐ Office Expenses
  - ☐ Deposit for Office Space
  - ☐ Rent for Office Space
  - ☐ Moving Expenses for Office Site Setup
- ☐ Bank Charges
- ☐ Telephone Expenses
  - ☐ Business Telephone Deposit
  - ☐ Business Telephone Installation
  - ☐ Monthly Charge for Business Telephone
  - ☐ Answering Machine and/or Personal Answering Service
  - ☐ Cell Phone and/or Pager

Checklist of Startup Costs

- ☐ Monthly Cell Phone Calling Plan
- ☐ Monthly Internet Connection, Fee Calculator

☐ Office Expenses and Supplies

- ☐ Computer
- ☐ Software
- ☐ Office Furniture: Desk, Chair, Cabinet, Shelf, or Bookcase
- ☐ Business Form Printing Business from Purchase
- ☐ Basic Office Supplies
- ☐ Pet sitting Supplies
- ☐ Office, Library Books, and Videos

☐ Advertising

- ☐ Web Site Design, Monthly Hosting
- ☐ Local Publications, Newspaper, Yellow Pages, Other
- ☐ Television, Radio

☐ Professional Affiliations and Subscriptions

- ☐ Annual Dues for Pet Sitters International, Chamber of Commerce, Pet-Related Organizations, Better Business Bureau
- ☐ Reference Books, Business-Related, Pet-Related, Other
- ☐ Magazine Subscriptions, Business-Related, Pet-Related, Other
- ☐ Convention Registration and Travel Miscellaneous

Sample Income Statement				
Period/Month	Month 1	Month 2	Month 3	Total
Income				$0
Sitting				$0
Other				$0
Total Sales	$0	$0	$0	$0
Operating Expenses				$0
Salaries and Wages				$0
Employee Benefits				$0
Payroll Taxes				$0
Rent				$0
Utilities				$0
Repairs and maintenance				$0
Insurance				$0
Travel				$0
Telephone				$0
Postage				$0
Office Supplies				$0
Advertising/Marketing				$0
Professional Fees				$0
Training and development				$0
Bank Charges				$0
Depreciation				$0
Miscellaneous				$0
Other				$0
Total Operating Expense	$0	$0	$0	$0
Operating Income	$0	$0	$0	$0
Interest Income (expense)				$0
Other income (expense)				$0
Total Non operating Income (expense)	$0	$)	$0	$0
Income (Loss) before taxes	$0	$0	$0	$0
Income Taxes				$0
Net Income (loss)	$0	$0	$0	$0
Cumulative Net Income (Loss)	$0	$0	$0	$0

Sample Invoice

Street: ____________________

Address: ____________________

Address 2: ____________________

City: ____________________ St: __________ Zip: __________

Phone: ____________________ Fax: ____________________

E-mail: ____________________

Statement

Statement #: ____________________

Date: ____________________

Customer ID: ____________________

Bill To:

Name: ____________________

Company Name: ____________________

Street Address: ____________________

Address 2: ____________________

City: ____________________ St: __________ Zip: __________

Date	Type	Invoice #	Description	Amount	Payment	Balance
					Total	$_______

Reminder: Please include the statement number on your check.

Terms: Balance due in 30 days.

Sample Remittance Slip

Customer Name: ____________________

Customer ID: ____________________

Statement #: ____________________

Date: ____________________

Amount Due: ____________________

Amount Enclosed: ____________________

Appendix C: Business Plan

Business Plan for a Startup Business

The business plan will help a business owner summarize the business, financial plan, and operation of a new business. The business plan will help you properly think through all the issues and decisions for your business, and avoid future problems.

If you request a loan or look for specialized insurance for your business, you may have to show the authority your business plan to ensure you have a viable strategy for your business.

In early chapters of this book, the factors that go into a business plan are discussed in detail. This template includes questions to help you formulate a plan, as well as financial worksheets. You may want to write the Executive Summary last, after putting together the rest of the business plan. If any of the questions do not apply to your business, simply skip them.

Business Plan

Owners: ______________________________

Business Name: ______________________________

Street Address ______________________________

Address 2: ______________________________

City: ________________ State _____ ZIP Code: __________

Telephone: ______________________________

Fax: ______________________________

E-mail: ______________________________

Table of Contents

Executive Summary

The executive summary should be written last and should contain all the information you wouldd tell someone about your business in a ten minute interview.

- What will your product be?
- Who will your customers be?
- Who are the owners?
- What do you think the future holds for your business and your industry?

Write the summary clearly and precisely so that it will be easy to read, but be sure to include your enthusiasm for your company.

General Company Description

What precisely is your business? What work will you do?

Mission Statement: What is your company's reason for existing? What are its' guiding principles?

Company Goals and Objectives: Where do you want your business to go? What do you want to achieve? What do you want your customers to experience?

Business Philosophy: What is important to you in business? Who are your target customers?

Describe your industry: Is it a growth industry? What changes do you foresee in the industry, short term and long term? How will you take advantage of those changes?

Legal form of ownership: Which legal form have you chosen: Sole proprietor, Partnership, Corporation, Limited liability corporation (LLC)? Why have you selected this form?

Products and Services

What are the pricing, fee, or leasing structures of your services?

Marketing Plan

Economics

- What is is your market size?
- How much of the market do you think you will have?
- Will you have a special niche in the market?

Current demand in target market

- What trends do you see in the pet sitting business? What do customers in your area prefer?

Growth potential and opportunity for a business of your size

- What barriers to entry do you face in entering this market with your new company?

Customers

- Who are your targeted customers?

- What are their characteristics?

Competition

- Who are your competitors?
- What do they offer in comparison to your business?
- How will your pet sitting services compare with the competition?
- Do you offer something that your competitors don't?

Niche

Now that you have systematically analyzed your industry, your product, your customers, and the competition, you should have a clear picture of where your company fits into the world.

In one short paragraph, define your niche — your unique corner of the market.

Strategy

Next, outline a marketing strategy that is consistent with your niche.

Promotion

- How will you get the word out to customers?

Advertising

- What media, why, and how often?
- What image do you want to project? How do you want customers to see you?

- How will you present your company's image (for example, things like logo design, cards and letterhead, brochures, and signs)?

Promotional Budget

- How much will you spend on the items listed above?

Pricing

- How will you set prices?
- What will be your customer service and credit policies?

Proposed Location

- Will you locate your business inside your home or at another location?

Sales Forecast

Once you have described your products, services, customers, markets, and marketing plans in detail, plan your sales for the year. A sales forecast spreadsheet can help you prepare a month-by-month projection. The forecast should be based on your historical sales, the marketing strategies that you have just described, your market research, and industry data, if available.

Operational Plan

- What is the daily operation of the business: its location, equipment, people, processes, and surrounding environment?

Legal Environment

- What are the licensing and bonding requirements for your business?

- Will you require any permits or special insurance to run your pet sitting business?
- What special regulations cover the industry (federal, state, or local level)?

Personnel

- How many employees will you have?
- Where and how will you find the right employees?
- What is the pay and benefits structure?
- How will you train them?
- Do you have schedules and written procedures prepared?

Credit Policies

- Do you plan to sell on credit?
- If yes, what policies will you have about who gets credit and how much?
- How will you check the creditworthiness of new customers?

Management and Organization

- Who will manage the business on a day-to-day basis?
- What experience does that person offer your business?

Startup Expenses and Capitalization

Your business financial plan should include an account of your expenses to start up the business, and the amount of money (capital) you have to run the business on day 1. In addition, it can be important to project your profits and loss for the first 12 months, to give yourself an idea what it will take to make a profit and be successful.

12-Month Profit and Loss Projection

Many business owners think of the 12-month profit and loss projection as the centerpiece of their plan. This is where you put it all together in numbers and get an idea of what it will take to make a profit and be successful.

Your sales projections will come from a sales forecast in which you forecast sales, cost of goods sold, expenses, and profit month-by-month for one year.

Four-Year Profit Projection (Optional)

The 12-month projection is the heart of your financial plan. This section is for those who want to carry their forecasts beyond the first year. Keep notes of your key assumptions, especially about things you expect will change dramatically after the first year.

Projected Cash Flow

Write down how much cash you need before startup for preliminary expenses, operating expenses, and reserves. Once your business is up and running, keep updating it and using it afterward. This projection is like a forward look at your checking account, helping you anticipate what profits you will have each month.

Opening Day Balance Sheet

A balance sheet shows what items of value are held by the company (assets), and what its debts are (liabilities). Use a startup expenses and capitalization spreadsheet as a guide to preparing a balance sheet as of opening day. Then detail how you calculated the account balances on your opening day balance sheet.

Conclusion

Here you need to summarize your business report.

"Our dogs will love and admire the meanest of us, and feed our colossal vanity with their uncritical homage."
~Agnes Repplier

Appendix D: Marketing Materials

Sample Press Release

For_Immediate_Release:

Title: Loving Pet Care for Holiday Travelers

(Release Date)

(City name/Release Date) — A professional dog walking and pet sitting service, (Business Name), now has service to cover the (coverage area) just in time for the holidays. (Owner Name) provides expert care as a licensed pet sitting professional.

"In home animal care is beneficial for both pets and their owners," says (Owner Name). "Animals do much better in their normal, safe, and secure environment while surrounded by familiar sights, sounds, and smells. They will receive love and personal attention and are able to stick to their normal routine while eliminating the trauma of an unfamiliar environment and exposure to other animals."

(Business Name) provides a variety of services for dogs, cats, and other small animals, including private and group dog walks and doggie play groups, cat visits, in-home overnight sitting, private boarding, day care, home care, and pet taxi.

The demand for professional pet sitting and dog-walking services is at an all-time high. Pet ownership is rising, pet owners are working longer hours and traveling more for business and personal reasons than ever before, and pet owners are

Sample Press Release

moving away from kenneling their pets because of health concerns, making alternatives like (Business Name) more attractive.

More information, a complete list of service areas and contact information are available at (Business Name) Web site at (Web site address) or by calling (phone number).

CONTACT:

(Business Name)

(Contact Name)

(Address)

(Phone)

(E-mail)

(Web site)

###

Sympathy Card for the Loss of a Pet

The following is a card that you can send to a client in the event that one of his or her pets dies.

For your company, you would need to place your logo where the ABC Petsitters Inc. logo is displayed. You can find the color artwork on the companion CD-ROM.

You can personalize your message for everyone you send it to. Save the card as a template on your computer and keep it as you need it. You can also use the card to send for other occasions.

You can easily make this card by folding a sheet of printing paper into quadrants (for a smaller card) or in half (for a larger card). For the best results, you may want to print it on a heavier card stock paper.

Front of Card

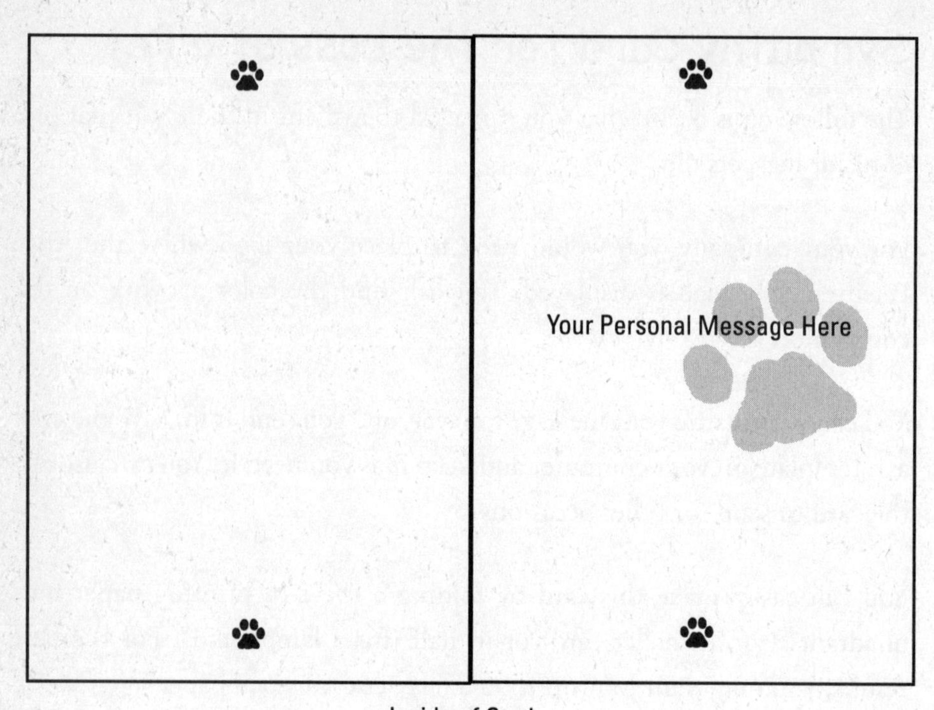

Inside of Card

Bibliography

This book was made possible through the excellent resources of a number of experts. I recommend the following books and sites for further reading.

Pet Sitters International (PSI™)
www.petsit.com

Professional United Petsitters, LLC
www.petsits.com

National Association of Professional Pet Sitters (NAPPS)
www.petsitters.org

International Llama Registry
www.lamaregistry.com

www.about.com/exotic pets

Entrepreneur Magazine's "*Start Your Own Pet-Sitting Business: Your Step-by-Step Guide*," Cheryl Kimball, Entrepreneur Press, 2005

Pet Sitting For Profit, 3rd Edition, Patti J. Moran and Michelle Boles, Howell Book House, 2006

The Professional Pet Sitter: Your Guide to Starting and Operating a Successful Service, Lori Mangold and Scott Mangold, Paws-itive Press, 2005

How to Start a Home-Based Pet Care Business, 2nd Edition, Kathy Salzberg, Globe Pequot, 2006

Author Biography

Angela Williams Duea

Angela Williams Duea is a freelance writer and animal lover. Her pets have included a German Shepherd, a Golden Retriever, six mixed-breed cats and one purebred Maine Coon cat, numerous salt- and fresh-water fish, and a salamander. Her writing has been published in numerous trade and commercial magazines, Web sites, and newsletters; her company is Pearl Writing Services at **www.pearlwriting.com**. This is her first book.

Angela lives in the Chicago area with her husband, Joseph, a former cattle rancher who contributed greatly to the farm animal information in this book. They have two teenage daughters and share their home with two slightly spoiled cats.

Index

C

D

E

F

G

H

I

W